North Carolina

BY THEME

DAY TRIPS

Marla Hardee Milling

Adventure Publications
Cambridge, Minnesota

Cover and book design by Jonathan Norberg

Front cover photo: Linn Cove Viaduct (photographed by Sean Pavone/Shutterstock)

Back cover photo: Chimney Rock (photographed by Jon Bilous/Shutterstock)

Photo credits as noted on page and as follows: Page 2: FXQuadro/Shutterstock; page 32: Gingo Scott/Shutterstock; page 37: Gingo Scott/Shutterstock; page 38: Jon Bilous/Shutterstock; page 44: ZakZeinert/Shutterstock; page 56: Nature Lovin' Geek/Shutterstock; page 59: Bryan Pollard/Shutterstock; page 66: Jeffrey M. Frank/Shutterstock; page 72: Jmturner/Wikimedia Commons/public domain; page 76: Christen Alley/Shutterstock; page 78: Studio ART/Shutterstock; page 89: EPG_EuroPhotoGraphics/Shutterstock; page 94: Nancy Bauer/Shutterstock; page 95: Marc Parsons/Shutterstock; page 96: NcikName/Shutterstock; page 113: Gingo Scott/Shutterstock; page 121: 1512 Creative/Shutterstock; page 131: digidreamgrafix/Shutterstock; page 137: David Byron Keener/Shutterstock; page 138: SNEHIT/Shutterstock; page 146: Cvandyke/Shutterstock; page 151: J.K. York/Shutterstock; page 152: Emily Tucker/Shutterstock; page 155: TheBigMK/Shutterstock; page 165: Gingo Scott/Shutterstock; page 171: Jeffrey M. Frank/Shutterstock; page 177: CeGe/Shutterstock; page 178: Harry Powell/Shutterstock; page 181: Danita Delmont/Shutterstock; page 187: jadimages/Shutterstock; page 188: starryvoyage/Shutterstock; page 191: Charles Chadwick Talton/Shutterstock.

10 9 8 7 6 5 4

North Carolina Day Trips by Theme

Published by Adventure Publications
An imprint of AdventureKEEN
310 Garfield Street South
Cambridge, Minnesota 55008
(800) 678-7006
adventurepublications.net

Printed in China
ISBN 978-1-59193-885-9 (pbk.); ISBN 978-1-59193-886-6 (ebook)

Table of Contents

Dedication

Dedicated to the memory of **Ruth Gardner Camblos,** 1921–2009

When I was in high school in the late 1970s, Ruth "Rudy" Camblos hired me to type her manuscripts as she was working on updates to her *'Round the Mountains* guidebook, which she first published, along with Virginia Winger, in 1972. She set up a work space for me in her Biltmore Forest home in Asheville. As the years went by, we stayed in touch, and Rudy would always ask me, "When are you going to write *your* book?" I wish she were here to know that this is my fourth nonfiction title. It is with great love that I dedicate this book to her memory.

Also dedicated to the memory of **Riley Howell,** 1997–2019

During the process of writing this book, I was deeply inspired by the heroism and selfless act of 21-year-old Riley Howell, a student at the University of North Carolina at Charlotte who tackled a gunman who entered his classroom on the last day of class, April 30, 2019. He exhibited the highest level of love as he sacrificed his own life to save the lives of others. I did not have the chance to meet Riley, but I felt as if I knew him from watching love blossom between him and his longtime girlfriend, Lauren Westmoreland. I learned about him through pictures, adventures, and stories posted on Facebook over the years by Lauren's parents and my friends, Amy and Kevin Westmoreland. Please join me in remembering and honoring Riley's incredible bravery by supporting the Riley Howell Foundation, rileyhowellfoundation.org.

Acknowledgments

My family tops the list when it comes to people to thank. I am very appreciative of the support and encouragement of my two children, Ben and Hannah; my dad, Ray Hardee; and my maternal aunt, May Shuford. I also appreciate the support of Craig Distl of Distl PR, Jan Schochet (insidercarolina.com), and all of the people I met and talked with across the great state of North Carolina as I wrote this book.

A special thanks to Karri Brantley for taking my author photo and to David Oakes and John Tissue, executive director of the Cherokee Historical Association, for help with photos.

While conducting research for this book, I explored sites from Murphy to Manteo—from exhilarating mountain peaks to the valleys below and eastward to the coastline.

I purposefully went to some of the places I've always wanted to visit but had never been before. I fell in love with one of those places—Mount Airy—on my first visit in late summer 2018; the people there are truly as friendly as the characters from Mayberry from *The Andy Griffith Show.* Griffith grew up in Mount Airy and modeled his popular show after the town and its residents. You'd be hard-pressed to find someone in North Carolina (and beyond) who doesn't nod and smile at the mention of Mayberry. A total of 249 episodes of the show aired on CBS from 1960 to 1968, and it remains a much-watched favorite in syndication.

I have to give a special shout-out to Mary Dowell, owner of the Snappy Lunch in Mount Airy, who treated me like an old friend the moment I walked into her diner. Here's some fun trivia: the Snappy Lunch is the only Mount Airy business Andy Griffith mentioned by name in an episode of *The Andy Griffith Show.*

A few months earlier, I had a chance to visit the Brinegar Cabin, a well-preserved mountain homestead on the Blue Ridge Parkway, which I had always wanted to see. I also retreated to many of my longtime favorite places, such as the Biltmore Estate, Wrightsville Beach, and Grandfather Mountain, and I took a repeat drive along the spectacular Linn Cove Viaduct, depicted on the cover of this book.

I extend my thanks to the team at Adventure Publications—Tim Jackson, Brett Ortler, Liliane Opsomer, and Andrea Bong—for giving me the opportunity to write this book. I also appreciate the keen eye of editor Amber Henderson.

Try a craft beer at one of the state's many breweries.

AT FIRST GLANCE, you might question planning a day trip around a tasty beverage. But in North Carolina, quite a few craft breweries offer music events and open spaces for families to play and have fun. While craft breweries seem to be a dime a dozen these days, I've focused on some that have become destinations, and I've also provided a listing of other breweries and wineries to explore in the state. Most have tasting rooms to sample their products, and many host special events.

A TASTE OF NORTH CAROLINA: Craft Beer, Wine, & Cider

1 Asheville Pizza & Brewing

675 Merrimon Ave., Asheville, NC 28804; 828-254-1281
ashevillebrewing.com

This place is a gold mine for family fun. It makes really tasty beers with special seasonal and event beers. Some of the mainstays include Rocket Girl Lager, Ninja Porter, and Shiva IPA. This site includes a movie theater featuring $3 movies, a full restaurant, and an arcade/party room. The company has two other locations that don't include the movies or games: 77 Coxe Ave., Asheville, NC 28801 (828-255-4077), and the delivery/carry-out-only location at 1850 Hendersonville Road, Ste. A, Asheville, NC 28803 (828-277-5775). All three locations offer growlers, six-packs, and 22-ounce bottles of its specialty in-house brews.

2 Green Man Brewery

27 Buxton Ave., Asheville, NC 28801; 828-252-5502
greenmanbrewery.com

One of Asheville's oldest breweries, it's evolved from a small space, known as Dirty Jack's, to a three-story, 20,000-square-foot place it calls a brewtique. An indoor/outdoor taproom on the top floor shows off the production facilities, while also providing stunning mountain views. Hour-long brewery tours are offered Thursday–Sunday for a small fee and include beer sampling.

3 Highland Brewing

12 Old Charlotte Hwy., Ste. 200, Asheville, NC 28803; 828-299-3370
highlandbrewing.com

In 1994 Oscar Wong founded Highland Brewing—the first brewery in Asheville since Prohibition. It started out in the basement of a business on Biltmore Avenue in downtown Asheville and eventually moved to its current location in east Asheville. Highland Brewing crafts a variety of beers, but its Cold Mountain release has reached almost cult status. The facility includes a tasting room and meadow for special events. It often brings in food trucks, bands, and other entertainment. Plus, it has an indoor event center that includes a main floor, mezzanine, and rooftop beer garden; all three levels are wheelchair accessible. The event center is available to rent for weddings, rehearsal dinners, meetings, networking events, and more. A pioneer of the craft beer movement in Asheville, Wong was one of the reasons Asheville was named Beer City U.S.A. for several years in an online poll.

4 Hi-Wire Brewing

Big Top: 2A Huntsman Pl., Asheville, NC 28803; 828-738-2448
South Slope: 197 Hilliard Ave., Asheville, NC 28801
Golden Belt: 800 Taylor St., #9-150, Durham, NC 27701
hiwirebrewing.com

Hi-Wire offers three locations—two in Asheville and one in Durham. The grandest of all is the Big Top location, encompassing 27,000 square feet of space for production and a taproom. It includes a beer garden and a permanent food truck and serves as a venue for large events. Private rentals of the facility are available. The Durham location, called Golden Belt, highlights games and activities, such as shuffleboard, table tennis, soccer pool, and more. A colorful mural wraps the room.

5 New Belgium

21 Craven St., Asheville, NC 28806; 828-333-6900
newbelgium.com/brewery/asheville

Live music and tours of the brewery are featured on the schedule here. The daily tours last an hour and a half and include beer sampling for those 21 and older; all ages are welcome on the tour, which is free but requires online reservations. A 2-hour Behind-the-Scenes Brewery Tour costs $200 for up to 10 guests (age 18 and up; must be at least 21 to sample the beer). A fun outdoor area allows families to gather and play together.

6 The Olde Mecklenburg Brewery

4150 Yancey Road, Charlotte, NC 28217; 704-525-5644
oldemeckbrew.com

Drink indoors or outdoors here. The expansive Brauhaus features a lively community atmosphere indoors, where German-style beers are paired with a variety of German fare. Outdoors, experience the Biergarten, filled with umbrella-shaded picnic tables in a serene setting. Check the calendar for special events, or book space for your own party or meeting. Free brewery tours are offered on Saturday and Sunday afternoons; registration is not required. Children are allowed on the tour if accompanied by an adult over the age of 21.

7 Oskar Blues Brewery

342 Mountain Industrial Dr., Brevard, NC 28712; 828-883-2337
oskarblues.com/breweries/brevard

Oskar Blues opened its North Carolina location in December 2012 with a batch of Dale's Pale Ale. The Tasty Weasel Taproom includes an outdoor patio bar, food truck service, and free brewery tours. Live music and outdoor activities are prevalent here.

8 Pisgah Brewing Company

150 Eastside Dr., Black Mountain, NC 28711; 828-669-0190
pisgahbrewing.com

The taproom—with its bar and courtyard seating, indoor stage, and outdoor stage—offers lots of space to unwind here. Pisgah Brewing offers year-round brews like the ever-popular Pisgah Pale Ale and Nitro Stout. It also produces craft seasonal varieties like Chocolatized and Leaf Amber Ale. The site hosts a steady flow of great concerts—check the website to see who will be performing next, as well as for ticket information and other details. Some of the shows are free, while others have a fee.

9 Sierra Nevada

100 Sierra Nevada Way, Mills River, NC 28732; 828-708-6242
sierranevada.com/brewery/north-carolina/taproom

This expansive space has quickly become a favorite for locals and visitors alike. The taproom serves 23 beers. The innovative restaurant—which includes a back porch area, beer garden, and the Mills River Estate Garden—highlights farm-to-table dishes. Live music is a mainstay here with the Taproom Concert Series; the outdoor amphitheater hosts free weekly music events. Tours fill up quickly—online reservations are required for all tours except the Guided Tastings and self-guided Visitor Corridor. The 45-minute Brewery Tour is offered free to people over the age of 12, but all other tours entail a fee.

10 Wilmington Brewing Company

824 S. Kerr Ave., Wilmington, NC 28403; 910-392-3315
wilmingtonbrewingcompany.com

John and Michelle Savard have developed a small home brew shop into an 11,800-square-foot facility and take pride in serving fresh beer straight from the tank. If you're thinking of brewing your own, this is the place to go—it sells all the supplies you need in its Homebrew Shop, with free advice. Or you can simply enjoy sampling their creations. The taproom features 15 rotating drafts. If everything goes according to plan, the owners will unveil a 5,000-square-foot venue by spring 2020 for large-scale events, live music, and private rentals.

A Few Other Breweries, Plus Wineries & Cideries

CRAFT BEER

Appalachian Mountain Brewery
163 Boone Creek Dr., Boone, NC 28607; 828-263-1111; amb.beer

Blowing Rock Brewery
152 Sunset Dr., Blowing Rock, NC 28605; 828-414-9600; blowingrockbrewing.com

Bond Brothers Beer Company
202 E. Cedar St., Cary, NC 27511; 919-459-2670; bondbrothersbeer.com

Burial Beer Co.
40 Collier Ave., Asheville, NC 28801; 828-475-2739
500 E. Davie St., Ste. 170, Raleigh, NC 27601; 919-617-1314; burialbeer.com

Crank Arm Brewing Company
319 W. Davie St., Raleigh, NC 27601; 919-324-3529; crankarmbrewing.com

Double Barley Brewing
3174 US 70 W, Smithfield, NC 27577; 919-934-3433; doublebarleybrewing.com

Fonta Flora Brewery
317 N. Green St., Morganton, NC 28655; 828-475-0153; fontaflora.com

Four Saints Brewing Company
218 S. Fayetteville St., Asheboro, NC 27203; 336-610-3722; foursaintsbrewing.com

Mother Earth Brewing
311 N. Heritage St., Kinston, NC 28501; 252-208-2437; motherearthbrewing.com

Nantahala Brewing Company
61 Depot St., Bryson City, NC 28713; 828-488-2337; nantahalabrewing.com

NoDa Brewing Company
2921 N. Tryon St., Charlotte, NC 28206; 704-900-6851; nodabrewing.com

VINEYARDS & CIDERIES

Banner Elk Winery
60 Deer Run Lane, Banner Elk, NC 28604; 828-898-9090
bannerelkwinery.com

Black Mountain Ciderworks + Meadery
104 Eastside Dr., Unit 307, Black Mountain, NC 28711; 828-419-0089
blackmountainciderworks.com

Bold Rock Hard Cider
72 School House Road, Mills River, NC 28759; 828-595-9941
boldrock.com

Burntshirt Vineyards
2695 Sugarloaf Road, Hendersonville, NC 28792; 828-685-2402
burntshirtvineyards.com

Childress Vineyards
1000 Childress Vineyard Road, Lexington, NC 27295; 336-236-9463
childressvineyards.com

Dennis Vineyards
24043 Endy Road, Albemarle, NC 28001; 704-982-6090
dennisvineyards.com

Duplin Winery
505 N. Sycamore St., Rose Hill, NC 28458; 800-774-9634
duplinwinery.com

Elkin Creek Vineyard
318 Elkin Creek Mill Road, Elkin, NC 28621; 336-526-5119
elkincreekvineyard.com

JOLO Winery & Vineyards
219 JOLO Winery Lane, Pilot Mountain, NC 27041; 336-614-0030
jolovineyards.com

Jones von Drehle Vineyards & Winery
964 Old Railroad Grade Road, Thurmond, NC 28683; 336-874-2800, ext. 3
jonesvondrehle.com

Point Lookout Vineyards
408 Appleola Road, Hendersonville, NC 28792; 828-808-8923
pointlookoutvineyards.com

Raffaldini Vineyards
450 Groce Road, Ronda, NC 28670; 336-835-9463
raffaldini.com

RagApple Lassie Vineyards
3724 RagApple Lassie Lane, Boonville, NC 27011; 336-367-6000
ragapplelassie.com

Round Peak Vineyards
765 Round Peak Church Road, Mount Airy, NC 27030; 336-352-5595
roundpeak.com

Sanders Ridge Vineyard & Winery
3200 Round Hill Road, Boonville, NC 27011; 336-677-1700
sandersridge.com

Shelton Vineyards
286 Cabernet Lane, Dobson, NC 27017; 336-366-4724
sheltonvineyards.com

Silver Fork Vineyard & Winery
5000 Patton Road, Morganton, NC 28655; 828-391-8783
silverforkwinery.com

Treehouse Vineyards
301 Bay St., Monroe, NC 28112; 704-283-4208
treehousevineyards.com

Urban Orchard Cider Co.
210 Haywood Road, Asheville, NC 28806; 828-774-5151
urbanorchardcider.com

The fried pork chop sandwich at Snappy Lunch comes with some unusual toppings. (photographed by Marla Milling)

WHEN IT COMES TO FOOD, North Carolina has plenty of bragging rights. It's home to such popular creations as Krispy Kreme Doughnuts, Mt. Olive Pickles, Bojangles' Famous Chicken 'n Biscuits, Texas Pete, Pepsi, Cheerwine, and more. I've selected a variety of popular food festivals and other notable culinary offerings where you can tour the facilities, sample the flavors, and also follow some food trails.

A TASTE OF NORTH CAROLINA: Foodie Delights

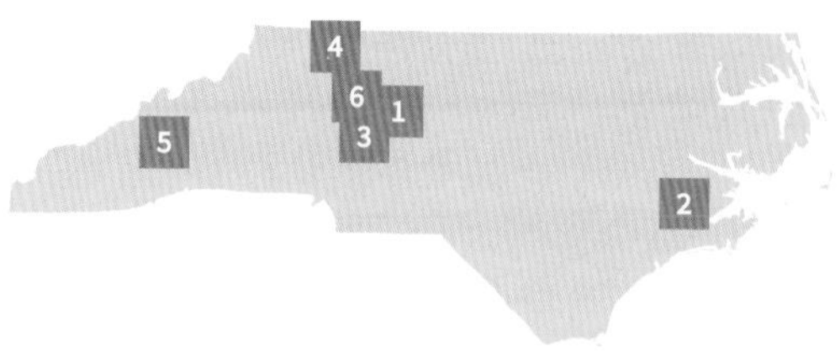

1 Barbecue Festival

Main St., Lexington, NC 27292; 336-956-1880
barbecuefestival.com

Barbecue is one of the most controversial food topics in North Carolina, as folks debate which one is best—barbecue created in the eastern part of the state or the western part. Decide for yourself at the popular Barbecue Festival, started in 1984 in Lexington, known as the Barbecue Capital of the World. *USA Today* at one time declared the festival "One of Ten Great Places to Celebrate Food." The festival is held each October.

2 Birthplace of Pepsi Store

256 Middle St., New Bern, NC 28560; 252-636-5898
pepsistore.com

New Bern is the birthplace of Pepsi-Cola. Caleb Bradham created the drink in 1893 at his drugstore and sold it under the name Brad's Drink. The name changed to Pepsi-Cola in 1898 to reflect the root of the word *dyspepsia* (of which Bradham believed Pepsi helped relieve symptoms) and the kola nuts used in the recipe. The Birthplace of Pepsi Store opened in 1998 to commemorate Pepsi's 100th birthday.

3 Cheerwine Festival

Downtown Salisbury, NC; 704-638-5294
cheerwinefest.com

A new soft drink came on the scene in 1917. Salisbury general store owner L. D. Peeler drew rave reviews with Cheerwine. It wasn't his first flavor. He had been successful selling Mint Cola, but a sugar shortage in World War II forced him to change direction. That's when he came up with the Cheerwine flavor. In 2017, on the occasion of the drink's 100th birthday, The Cheerwine Company joined with the City of Salisbury to create a Cheerwine Festival. It's held in May each year.

4 Famous Pork Chop Sandwich at Snappy Lunch

125 N. Main St., Mount Airy, NC 27030; 336-786-4931
thesnappylunch.com

I'll admit that I had some hesitation when I heard about the unusual mixture of ingredients on this sandwich, but for the sake of research I told Snappy Lunch owner Mary Dowell that I wanted to try one all the way. I'm so glad I did. It's amazing. Her late husband, Charles Dowell, created the Famous Pork Chop Sandwich—a fried pork chop topped with chili, coleslaw, mustard, onion, and tomato.

5 French Broad Chocolate

Chocolate Lounge and Boutique: 10 S. Pack Square, Asheville, NC 28801; 828-252-4181
Factory & Cafe: 821 Riverside Dr., Ste. 199, Asheville, NC 28801; 828-348-5169
Cookies & Creamery: 21 Buxton Ave., Asheville, NC 28801; 828-348-5323
frenchbroadchocolates.com

There are a couple of ways to savor the offerings of French Broad Chocolate. The first is as easy as stopping in at its Pack Square location in downtown Asheville and picking out some of its artisan truffles, chocolate bars, and other items. Or you can head to its factory to see the process in action. Hour-long tours are offered Saturday–Sunday, with 30-minute tours available Monday–Friday (reservations and a small fee required). The tour includes a guided sampling. Cookies & Creamery opened in 2019 in the company's former factory space on Buxton Avenue and features signature truffles, sundaes, shakes, espresso drinks, and even floats crafted with beer and cider.

6 Mrs. Hanes' Hand-Made Moravian Cookies

4643 Friedberg Church Road, Clemmons, NC 27012; 336-764-1402
hanescookies.com

Tradition is closely followed here. The company uses an age-old family recipe and rolls and cuts each cookie by hand, just like the family's ancestors did generations ago, and then the tins are hand packed. Six flavors are available: sugar, ginger, lemon, chocolate, butterscotch, and black walnut. Tours/tastings are available January–October for a small fee; reservations are required.

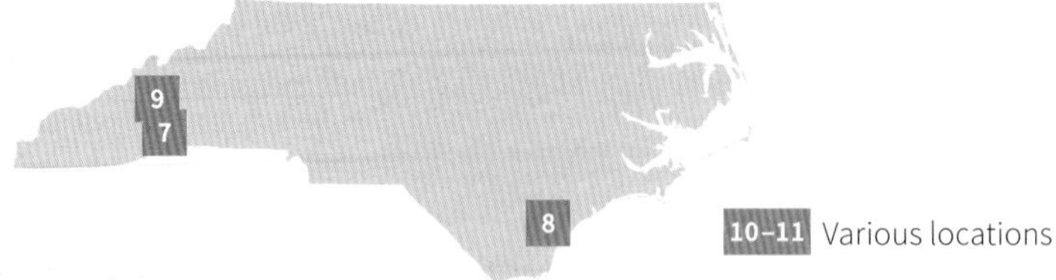

7 North Carolina Apple Festival

Main St., Hendersonville, NC 28792; 828-697-4557
ncapplefestival.org

This festival has been delighting apple lovers for more than 70 years. It features four days of activities (ending with a Labor Day parade) on Main Street in Hendersonville, as well as opportunities for buying apples and apple products directly from Henderson County growers, enjoying live entertainment, and browsing handmade arts and crafts. More than 65% of all the apples grown in North Carolina are cultivated within Henderson County, which has about 200 growers in all.

8 North Carolina Blueberry Festival

106 E. Wilmington St., Burgaw, NC 28425; 910-259-2007
ncblueberryfestival.com

Held on the third Saturday of June each year, this festival draws more than 30,000 visitors to the town of Burgaw. Along with blueberries, the event features a recipe contest, barbecue cook-off, car show, street fair, and special exhibits.

9 Omni Grove Park Inn National Gingerbread House Competition

290 Macon Ave., Asheville, NC 28804; 800-413-5778
tinyurl.com/natlgingerbreadomni

Gingerbread houses take center stage each holiday season at the Omni Grove Park Inn, as culinary artists from around the country (kids and adults) craft whimsical, traditional, and elaborate gingerbread houses for competition and display. The public is welcome to view the displays for free (Fridays and Saturdays are reserved for hotel guests only, and non-hotel guests are requested to visit during non-peak times). There is a fee for parking, with a portion of the proceeds going to area nonprofits.

10 Surry Sonker Trail

Various locations in Surry County; 800-948-0949
sonkertrail.org

A sonker is a delicious dessert that's sort of a cross between a pie and a deep-dish cobbler. Sonkers may be filled with a variety of fruits, such as peaches, raspberries, blackberries, or apples. Others are made with sweet potatoes. Some people in Surry County refer to the dish as a zonker. There are currently six locations on the Surry Sonker Trail map (free for download online). Plus, a Sonker Festival is held each year on the first Saturday in October at the Edwards-Franklin House, located just west of Mount Airy.

11 WNC Cheese Trail

Various locations in Western North Carolina; 828-484-1586
wnccheesetrail.org

Traveling along this tasty trail is a fun way to explore Western North Carolina while coming into direct contact with some of the area's cheese makers. They started this trail in 2012 and also host the Carolina Mountain Cheese Fest. There are almost a dozen sites to visit. Check the website for a map, as well as for individual business websites and hours.

Other Tasty Festivals

BBQ Fest on the Neuse
Pearson Park, 210 W. Gordon St., Kinston, NC 28501; 252-527-1131
kinstonbbq.com

Carolina Donut Festival
Downtown Marion, NC; 828-659-7132
carolinadonutfestival.com

Carolina Strawberry Festival
Downtown Wallace, NC; 910-447-9925
carolinastrawberryfestival.com

Grifton Shad Festival
485 Queen St., Grifton, NC 28530
griftonshadfestival.com

NC Oyster Festival
8 E. Second St., Ocean Isle Beach, NC 28469; 910-754-6644
ncoysterfestival.com

N.C. Peach Festival
214 S. Main St., Candor, NC 27229; 910-974-4221
ncpeachfestival.com

North Carolina Pickle Festival

123 N. Center St., Mount Olive, NC 28365; 919-658-3113
ncpicklefest.org

North Carolina Seafood Festival

113 Arendell St., Morehead City, NC 28557; 252-726-6273
ncseafoodfestival.org

Smithfield Ham & Yam Festival

200 S. Front St., Smithfield, NC 27577; 919-934-0887
hamandyam.com

Sneads Ferry Shrimp Festival

126 Park Lane, Sneads Ferry, NC 28460
sneadsferryshrimpfestival.org

Winterville Watermelon Festival

324 Sylvania St., Winterville, NC 28590
watermelonfest.com

The National Gingerbread House Competition at Omni Grove Park Inn
(photographed by Marla Milling)

The grave of William Sydney Porter (also known as O. Henry, who wrote "The Gift of the Magi") at Riverside Cemetery (photographed by Marla Milling)

YOU CAN'T GO FAR in North Carolina without crossing paths with a writer. This state has inspired the work of many notable authors, including Asheville's most famous son, Thomas Wolfe. When Wolfe was a boy, his mother ran a boardinghouse, known as the Old Kentucky Home, and it's open for tours. There are also other places to explore with an eye out for literary connections.

BOOKS, MOVIES, & MUSIC:

Literary Landmarks & Bookstores

1 Carl Sandburg Home National Historic Site

81 Carl Sandburg Lane, Flat Rock, NC 28731; 828-693-4178
nps.gov/carl

Carl Sandburg, the Pulitzer Prize–winning poet and biographer of President Abraham Lincoln, enjoyed the inspiration he found living in Western North Carolina. He spent much of his life in the Midwest but retreated to the beauty of Flat Rock during the last phase of his life. The house where he and his family lived is open for tours. It underwent a massive renovation—every item was taken out of the home and stored while repairs and updates were finished. Everything was put back in place in late 2018. Make sure to check out the goat barns to see descendants of Lilian Sandburg's prize-winning goats and take time to enjoy the hiking trails. Closed January 1, Thanksgiving, and December 25; free admission, with a small fee for house tours.

2 Omni Grove Park Inn

290 Macon Ave., Asheville, NC 28804; 800-438-5800
omnihotels.com/hotels/asheville-grove-park

Famed author F. Scott Fitzgerald spent the summers of 1935 and 1936 living in rooms 441 and 443. He tried desperately to write profitable material but fell short in his efforts during that time. He moved his wife, Zelda, to nearby Highland Hospital, where she ultimately died in a fire many years later. It's fascinating to walk through this historic inn and imagine what life was like in Fitzgerald's day. The hotel also has shops and restaurants.

3 Riverside Cemetery

53 Birch St., Asheville, NC 28801; 828-350-2066
ashevillenc.gov/departments/parks/inventory/riverside_cemetery.htm

This beautiful, serene cemetery in Asheville's Montford neighborhood is the final resting place of authors Thomas Wolfe and William Sydney Porter, who wrote under the pseudonym O. Henry. Visitors often leave pens and pencils beside Wolfe's tombstone, and at Porter's grave they leave coins to represent $1.87, the amount of money Della had managed to save to buy her husband a Christmas gift in the short story "The Gift of the Magi." Stop by the cemetery office for a map of how to get to these graves, as well as the grave sites of other notable Asheville citizens.

4 Thomas Wolfe Memorial State Historic Site

52 N. Market St., Asheville, NC 28801; 828-253-8304
wolfememorial.com

When Thomas Wolfe's novel *Look Homeward, Angel* came out in October 1929, many people in Asheville were outraged. Even though he called it fiction, his work was a thinly veiled account of life in his hometown and the people he met growing up in his mother's boardinghouse. Today, the home is open for tours. It's not quite the same as when the Wolfe family inhabited it. An arsonist ignited the historic home in 1998, destroying the dining room and causing heavy damage. The building went through an extensive renovation but lost some of its timeworn patina as a historic home. Browse the exhibits in the visitor center. Closed Sunday, Monday, January 1, Good Friday, July 4, Veterans Day, Thanksgiving, day after Thanksgiving, and December 24–26. Admission charged.

5 Town of Blowing Rock

blowingrock.com/mitford

Novelist Jan Karon put Blowing Rock on the map with her books about Father Tim and other residents of Mitford, which is modeled after Blowing Rock. Her novels began when she started writing the Mitford stories as installments for the local paper, *The Blowing Rocket*. Readership soared and her stories became popular novels—14 in all, plus a book of prayers, a Mitford cookbook, and other books.

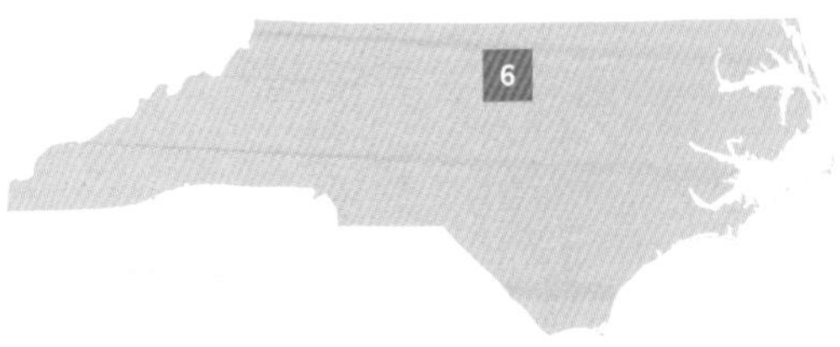

6 Town of Hillsborough

visithillsboroughnc.com

Hillsborough is a small town with a great advantage. It's located within 20 minutes or so of the campuses of the University of North Carolina at Chapel Hill and Duke University. Perhaps that's why there's such a large collection of writers and other creative souls who call this historic town home. A few of the notable authors who live here include Allan Gurganus, who wrote *Oldest Confederate Widow Tells All;* Annie Dillard (*Pilgrim at Tinker Creek*); Jill McCorkle (*Life After Life*); Lee Smith (*On Agate Hill*); Frances Mayes (*Under the Tuscan Sun*); Randall Kenan (*The Fire This Time*); and many others. Check the local bookstore Purple Crow Books (purplecrowbooks .com) for signed copies and special events.

BOOKSTORES

Battery Park Book Exchange
1 Page Ave., #101, Asheville, NC 28801; 828-252-0020
batteryparkbookexchange.com

Bookmarks
634 W. Fourth St., #110, Winston-Salem, NC 27101; 336-747-1471
bookmarksnc.org

City Center Gallery & Books
112 Hay St., Fayetteville, NC 28301; 910-678-8899
citycentergallery.com

City Lights Bookstore
3 E. Jackson St., Sylva, NC 28779; 828-586-9499
citylightsnc.com

The Country Bookshop
140 NW Broad St., Southern Pines, NC 28387; 910-692-3211
thecountrybookshop.biz

Curiosity Shop Books & Gifts
46 Valley River Ave., Murphy, NC 28906; 828-835-7433
murphybookstore.com

Malaprop's Bookstore/Cafe
55 Haywood St., Asheville, NC 28801; 828-254-6734
malaprops.com

McIntyre's Books
2000 Fearrington Village Center, Pittsboro, NC 27312; 919-542-3030
fearrington.com/mcintyres-books

The Next Chapter Books and Art
320 S. Front St., New Bern, NC 28560; 252-633-5774
thenextchapternc.com

Park Road Books
4139 Park Road, Charlotte, NC 28209; 704-525-9239
parkroadbooks.com

Purple Crow Books
109 W. King St., Hillsborough, NC 27278; 919-732-1711
purplecrowbooks.com

Quail Ridge Books
4209-100 Lassiter Mill Road, Raleigh, NC 27609; 919-828-1588
quailridgebooks.com

Wally's Service Station, a replica of the one in *The Andy Griffith Show,* located in Mount Airy (courtesy of Distl PR)

SO MANY MOVIES AND TV SHOWS have been filmed in North Carolina that you might want to tie your next day trip excursion to sites where many famous scenes appeared on the big screen. The city of Wilmington has even earned the moniker Hollywood East. There are also spots you can explore across North Carolina where such movies as *The Hunger Games* series, *The Last of the Mohicans, Forrest Gump,* and *Dirty Dancing* took shape.

BOOKS, MOVIES, & MUSIC:

Movie & TV Locales

1 Asheville

exploreasheville.com; 828-258-6129

One of the earliest movies that used Asheville as a setting was the silent film *Conquest of Canaan,* produced in 1921. It showcases the Asheville of yesteryear, with many buildings having now been replaced by others. The movie portrays Pack Square, the trolley cars that once traveled through town, the original Pack Memorial Library, and other locations. Robert Mitchum came to Asheville in 1957 to star in *Thunder Road* (1958). Many local residents were cast as extras in the movie, with scenes filmed around the area. Modern-day movies shot in Asheville include *Bull Durham* (1988) (which used McCormick Field as a location) and *Masterminds* (2016), about a Loomis Fargo heist. In *Masterminds* several segments were filmed around town, including a scene at the end of the movie where stars Zach Galifianakis and Kristen Wiig are sitting on the steps of the Buncombe County Courthouse.

2 Biltmore Estate

1 Lodge St., Asheville, NC 28803; 800-411-3812
biltmore.com

George Vanderbilt's 250-room mansion in Asheville has appeared in countless movies, with scenes shot inside the house as well as on the grounds. *Tap Roots,* starring Van Heflin and Susan Hayward, was filmed on the estate in 1947. Grace Kelly played the lead in one of her last movies, *The Swan* (1956), at Biltmore Estate before marrying Prince Rainier III of Monaco. Peter Sellers starred in *Being There* in 1979, Tim Conway and Don Knotts roamed the mansion's corridors searching for clues in *The Private Eyes* (1980), Jim Belushi came to Biltmore to perform in *Mr. Destiny* (1990), and Macaulay Culkin portrayed billionaire *Ri¢hie Ri¢h* in a 1994 movie based on the eponymous comic books. Other movies filmed at Biltmore include scenes of *The Last of the Mohicans,* featuring Daniel Day-Lewis and Madeleine Stowe (1992); *My Fellow Americans* (1996), starring Jack Lemmon and James Garner; *Patch Adams* (1998) with Robin Williams; *Hannibal* (2000) with Anthony Hopkins in a sequel to *The Silence of the Lambs;* and *The Odd Life of Timothy Green* (2012), showcasing Jennifer Garner and Joel Edgerton.

3 Blowing Rock

6570 Blue Ridge Pkwy., Blowing Rock, NC 28605; 828-295-2049
southernhighlandguild.org/shops-and-fairs/moses-cone-manor

Portions of *The Green Mile,* featuring Tom Hanks and Michael Clarke Duncan, were filmed at Flat Top Manor, the former home of textile magnate Moses Cone and his wife, Bertha. In the movie, it serves as a nursing home called Georgia Pines. The rest of the movie was shot in Tennessee. If you want a closer look at this historic home, located at milepost 294 along the Blue Ridge Parkway, the house serves as the Parkway Craft Center of the Southern Highland Craft Guild, and the grounds are open for walking and horseback riding.

4 Chimney Rock State Park

743 Chimney Rock Park Road, Chimney Rock, NC 28720; 828-625-1823
ncparks.gov/chimney-rock-state-park

The Last of the Mohicans (1992) was shot at several locations around Western North Carolina, but the final 17 minutes of the movie showcase the towering cliffs and Hickory Nut Falls in Chimney Rock State Park. Actress Drew Barrymore played the lead in a movie adaptation of Stephen King's novel *Firestarter* (1984), where Chimney Rock's front entrance gate and bridge show up on-screen. And the 1984 drama *A Breed Apart,* with Kathleen Turner, Rutger Hauer, and Powers Boothe, shows some of Chimney Rock's wooded areas and trails.

5 Dillsboro

gsmr.com; 800-872-4681

In the 1993 film *The Fugitive,* starring Harrison Ford, one pivotal scene involved his character's escape when a freight train plowed into the transport bus in which he was riding. That massive crash was staged in Dillsboro on a stretch of the Great Smoky Mountains Railroad using a real train and a real bus. Remnants of the wreck are visible today. From Haywood Road look down the bank to catch a glimpse of the abandoned film set. Another way to see the wreckage is to book a Tuckasegee River Excursion on the Great Smoky Mountains Railroad. It's a 4-hour ride from Bryson City to Dillsboro and back again and provides a view of the wreckage.

6 DuPont State Recreational Forest

89 Buck Forest Road, Cedar Mountain, NC 28718; 828-877-6527
ncforestservice.gov/contacts/dsf.htm

Fans of *The Hunger Games* series will enjoy exploring the beauty of DuPont State Recreational Forest, where some of the movie's scenes were filmed. This area has some amazing waterfalls, trails for mountain bikers and hikers, and fishing streams. Scenes to look for: Katniss's pond, the riverbank where Peeta camouflaged himself, and traces of pyrotechnics from the fireball sequence. Specific locations used in the movie include spots at the top of Triple Falls and along Little River. Tours are offered at hungergamesunofficialfantours.com. DuPont also served as the locale for portions of other movies: *The Last of the Mohicans, The Legacy of a Whitetail Deer Hunter, Seven Days Till Midnight,* and others.

7 Fontana Lake and Robbinsville

A remote section of Fontana Lake served as the backdrop for the 1994 film *Nell,* starring Jodie Foster and Liam Neeson. Other scenes were filmed in nearby Robbinsville. The Cherokee Hiking Club has information online about how to find the trail to the site of Nell's cabin: cherokeehikingclub.org/nells%20cabin.pdf. The 3.8-mile round trip leads to where the cabin once stood. All that's left now are foundation stones; the U.S. Forest Service demolished it due to safety concerns.

8 Grandfather Mountain

2050 Blowing Rock Hwy., Linville, NC 28646; 800-468-7325
grandfather.com

There's a long running sequence in the movie *Forrest Gump,* when Forrest (played by Tom Hanks) decides to go for a run "for no particular reason." That run continued for more than three years, showing Forrest at different locales across the country. If you head up to Grandfather Mountain, a marker on a winding stretch of road reads FORREST GUMP CURVE. A portion of that running scene was filmed here.

The home of Katniss Everdeen from *The Hunger Games* series at Henry River Mill Village (photographed by Marla Milling)

9 Henry River Mill Village

4255 Henry River Road, Hickory, NC 28602; 828-471-4768
henryrivermillvillage.com

This abandoned village between the towns of Morganton and Hickory served as the site of the dystopian community of District 12 in *The Hunger Games* movies. Notably, one of the former mill-worker cabins was transformed into the home of Katniss Everdeen, and the old general store became the bakery owned by Peeta Mellark's family in the movie. Calvin Reyes, along with his mother and stepfather, bought the 72-acre overgrown, desolate village in October 2017. They are working to transform the cabins into overnight accommodations, as well as add a restaurant, banquet hall, and wedding venue in the general store, once they renovate it. A steady flow of visitors comes to this site to see where *The Hunger Games* movies were filmed. Reservations required; closed Tuesday and Thursday, November–April; also closed Easter, July 4, Thanksgiving, and December 25. Admission is charged, and behind-the-scenes and unofficial Hunger Games tours that take you inside some of the buildings are offered for an additional fee.

10 Lake Lure

Morse Park Meadows, 2932 Memorial Hwy., Lake Lure, NC 28746
dirtydancingfestival.com

The iconic movie *Dirty Dancing,* showcasing the moves of Patrick Swayze and Jennifer Grey, has long been a fan favorite. It's depicted as taking place at Kellerman's Resort in the Catskills of New York, but it was actually shot in Virginia and North Carolina. Several locations around Lake Lure—including a boys' camp that served as staff cabins and a local gymnasium where Baby and Johnny performed their

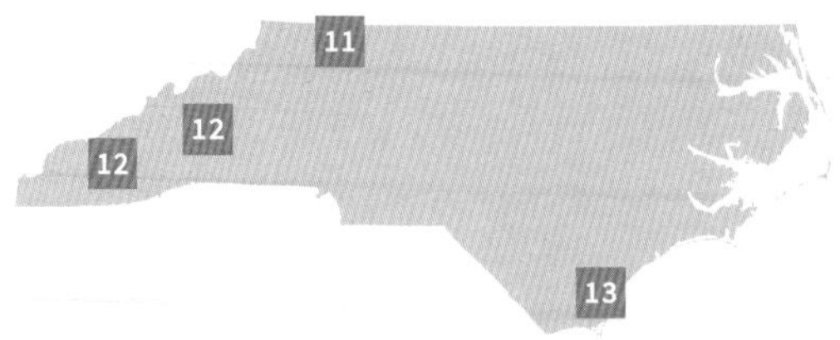

awe-inspiring dance—were used in the movie. Those sites no longer exist, but Lake Lure does host the Dirty Dancing Festival, which offers two days of fun each September, including a Lake Lift Competition reflective of one of the movie's most memorable scenes.

11 Mount Airy and The Andy Griffith Museum

218 Rockford St., Mount Airy, NC 27030; 336-786-1604
surryarts.org/agmuseum

Episodes of *The Andy Griffith Show* weren't shot in Andy's hometown of Mount Airy, but Mount Airy is a great day trip for those who love watching reruns and remembering when life was a bit simpler. The Andy Griffith Museum features props, clothing, and artifacts from the show, along with video clips and other memorabilia related to Andy Griffith's life and career. Many of the collected items were donated to the museum by Andy's boyhood friend, Emmett Forrest. Open daily, year-round; closed Thanksgiving and December 25. Admission charged. To get the full Mayberry experience, stop in for a meal at Snappy Lunch (see page 13), book a Squad Car Tour (much like the one Deputy Sheriff Barney Fife drove) and ride through the streets of Mount Airy (336-789-6743; tourmayberry.com), visit a replica courthouse and jail, and even book a night's stay in Griffith's boyhood home at 711 E. Haymore St. (336-789-5999).

12 Sylva, Dillsboro, Maggie Valley, and Black Mountain

visitnc.com/story/qzFT/behind-the-scenes-of-three-billboards-outside-ebbing-missouri

No offense to Missouri, but the beautiful landscape in the movie *Three Billboards Outside Ebbing, Missouri,* was distinctly North Carolina. Frances McDormand and Sam Rockwell both won Oscars for their performances. A day trip through the towns of Sylva, Dillsboro, and Maggie Valley will lead fans to some of the movie's scene locales. Visit Sassy Frass in Sylva—it's a consignment/gift shop that became the Ebbing Police Department in the movie; a food and wine shop in Dillsboro became the workplace for Mildred Hayes (McDormand's character); and J. Arthur's Restaurant in Maggie Valley hit the big screen as the setting for Mildred's dinner with James. The town of Black Mountain had a pretty big role because that's where the three billboards were located. They have since been removed, but you can go to the Town Pump Tavern, which was Ebbing's local bar in the movie. Also shot in Black Mountain at a conference center—*28 Days* (2000), starring Sandra Bullock. The center transformed into a drug and alcohol rehabilitation facility for the movie.

13 Wilmington

877-406-2356
wilmingtonandbeaches.com

Known as Hollywood East, Wilmington qualifies as the busiest moviemaking place in the state. It has served as the location for multiple TV series, independent productions, and other films. TV shows have included *Matlock* (starring Andy Griffith), *Dawson's Creek, One Tree Hill, Under the Dome, Homeland,* and *Swamp Thing.* Movies shot in and around Wilmington include *Iron Man 3, We're the Millers, The Conjuring, The Secret Life of Bees, Nights in Rodanthe, Divine Secrets of the Ya-Ya Sisterhood, A Walk to Remember, Muppets from Space, Weekend at Bernie's,* and dozens more. I recommend taking the Hollywood Location Walk tour to see a variety of sites and learn anecdotes about the actors and the productions from experienced guides. You can book a tour at hauntedwilmington.com/hollywood-location-walk.html.

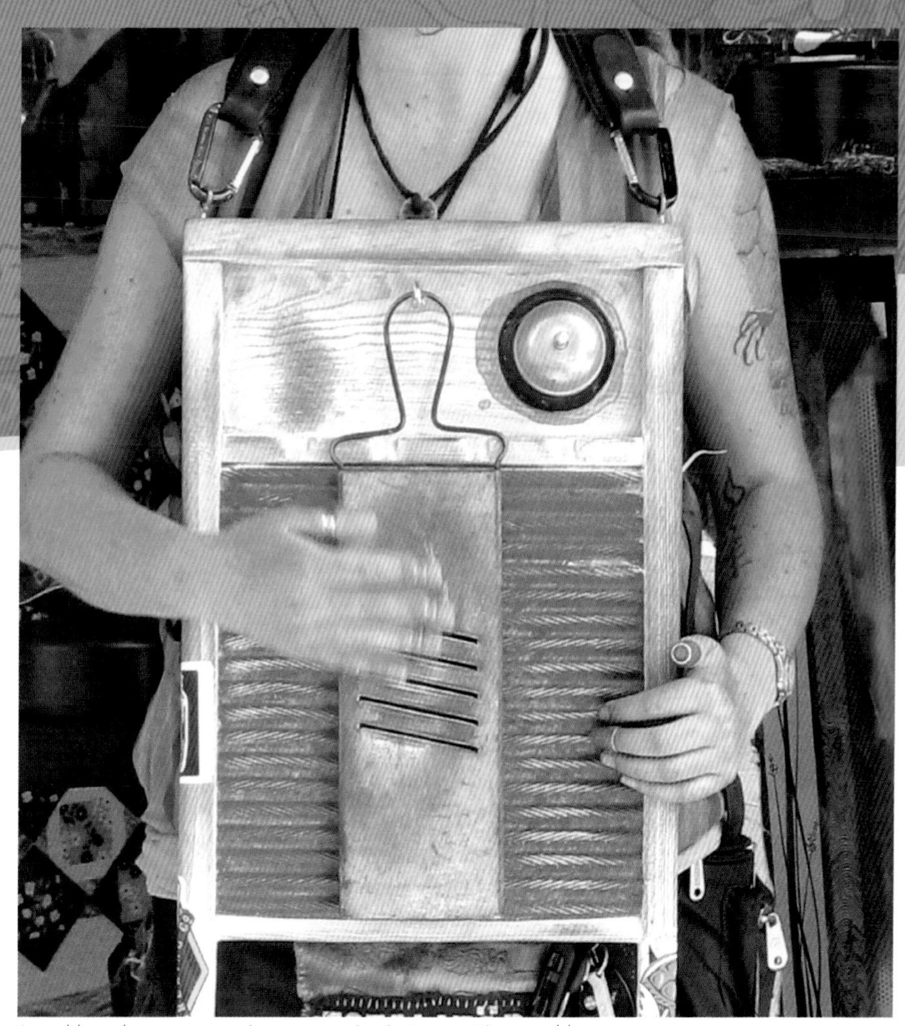
A washboard serves as a unique percussion instrument in some bluegrass acts.

LISTEN. Do you hear banjos playing? No, I'm not talking about the soundtrack of the movie *Deliverance*. I'm talking about the wealth of old-time music in North Carolina that continues to delight listeners. It's more than just banjos—you'll also hear fiddles, guitars, dulcimers, mandolins, and other instruments at concerts, jam sessions, and festivals around the state. To learn more about the state's tradition of old-time music, visit the website for the Blue Ridge Music Trails (blueridgemusicnc.com), which has descriptions of the instruments, jam etiquette, profiles of musicians and singers, and a link to a podcast.

BOOKS, MOVIES, & MUSIC:

Old-Time Music

1 Appalachian State Old-Time Fiddlers Convention

263 Locust St., Boone, NC 28608; 828-262-2000
fiddle.appstate.edu

This annual event held each February on the campus of Appalachian State University features concerts, instructional workshops, competitions, and a handmade craft market. This two-day convention takes place in the Plemmons Student Union.

2 Bascom Lamar Lunsford "Minstrel of Appalachia" Festival

Mars Hill University, 100 Athletic St., Mars Hill, NC 28754; 828-689-1115
mhu.edu/event/bascom-lamar-lunsford-minstrel-of-appalachia-festival

Bascom Lamar Lunsford's name is synonymous with the rich tradition of old-time music in North Carolina. A musician and a folklorist, he is credited with starting Asheville's Mountain Dance and Folk Festival. He collected and preserved Southern Appalachian music in the Library of Congress and promoted folk festivals, earning him the nickname Minstrel of the Appalachians. He was born in a house in Madison County located near what's now the campus of Mars Hill University. Each October, the university hosts the Bascom Lamar Lunsford "Minstrel of Appalachia" Festival with concerts; open jam sessions; a ballad swap; and workshops in fiddle, banjo, and guitar.

3 Bluff Mountain Festival

Hot Springs Resort and Spa, 315 Bridge St., Hot Springs, NC 28743; 828-649-1301
madisoncountyarts.com/events/bluff-mountain-music-festival

Musicians flock to this Madison County festival located on the grounds of the Hot Springs Spa and Resort each June. Bring blankets and lawn chairs for seating near the concert stage. The festival is free and also offers arts and crafts, food, and clogging.

4 Earl Scruggs Center: Music & Stories from the American South

103 S. Lafayette St., Shelby, NC 28150; 704-487-6233
earlscruggscenter.org

Banjo master Earl Scruggs grew up in Cleveland County. He's famous for a three-finger style of playing that's known far and wide as Scruggs's Style. This center bearing his name tells Scruggs's life story with interesting exhibits. It also hosts concerts and other events. Closed Sunday, Monday, January 1, Memorial Day, July 4, Labor Day, Thanksgiving, day after Thanksgiving, and December 24–25. Admission charged.

5 Feed & Seed

3715 Hendersonville Road, Fletcher, NC 28732; 828-216-3492
feedandseednc.com

Since 2007, this historical building has served as a fun, old-time music venue. The atmosphere of the building flashes back to a previous time, with its hammered tin ceiling tiles, hardwood floors, and 12-foot ceilings. It also functions as a cultural center for the Fletcher community, providing space for meetings, book clubs, and other events. Music begins at 7:30 p.m. on Friday and Saturday; no cover charge but donations appreciated.

6 MerleFest

1328 S. Collegiate Dr., Wilkesboro, NC 28697; 800-343-7857
merlefest.org

Created in 1988 to honor the memory of Eddy Merle Watson, the son of famed musician Doc Watson, MerleFest is held each April on the grounds of Wilkes Community College in Wilkesboro. Merle died in a tragic tractor accident at his Lenoir farm in 1985. The four-day event features 13 stages filled with premier musicians in the categories of old-time music, bluegrass, country, blues, rock, and other styles. A variety of ticket options, including by the day or admission for the full festival, are available.

7 Mountain Gateway Museum

24 Water St., Old Fort, NC 28762; 828-668-4626
mgmnc.org

Fun jam sessions presenting bluegrass and old-time string band music take place on most Sunday afternoons. Visitors are welcome to bring

their instruments and play along. In warm weather, you'll find them on the porch of the main building. On days when the weather is colder or rainy, they move indoors. Museum is closed Monday, January 1, Good Friday, July 4, Veterans Day, Thanksgiving, day after Thanksgiving, and December 24–26. Free admission; donations appreciated.

8 Mount Airy Blue Grass and Old-Time Fiddlers Convention

Veterans Memorial Park, 691 W. Lebanon St., Mount Airy, NC 27030; 336-345-7388
surryarts.org/mafiddlersconvention

Held annually in June, this convention is dedicated to old-time music, bluegrass, and dance. Started in 1972, it features two full days of jam sessions, competitions, dancing, and singing. The event takes place rain or shine—bring along a blanket or chair for outdoor seating if the weather is nice. Admission charged.

9 Shindig on the Green

Pack Square Park, 80 Court Plaza, Asheville, NC 28801; 828-258-6101, ext. 345
folkheritage.org/asheville-events/shindig-on-the-green

Take a chair or blanket to Pack Square Park "along about sundown" on most Saturdays in July and August and enjoy a long-running concert of old-time music, ballad singing, clogging, and storytelling. The main performances take place on the Bascom Lamar Lunsford Stage, but impromptu jam sessions can be found around the periphery. The Folk Heritage Committee, which produces Shindig, is also responsible for the Mountain Dance and Folk Festival, held in August. The festival is a ticketed event, while Shindig is free of charge.

10 Todd Mercantile

3899 Todd Railroad Grade Road, Todd, NC 28684; 336-877-5401
toddmercantile.com/live-events

Old-time musicians gather together every Saturday at the Todd Mercantile. This ongoing free event takes place 1–3 p.m. It's held on the front porch.

Find a jam session or festival to enjoy the sound of fiddles and banjos.

The Harvey B. Gantt Center for African-American Arts + Culture (in the background) sits across the street from the Mint Museum Uptown.

ART LOVERS WILL DELIGHT in the wide array of holdings in museums across the state. North Carolina celebrates a vast expression of creativity, from works by some of the most influential artists to masterful frescoes and contemporary decorative arts.

HISTORIC SITES & MUSEUMS:

Art Museums

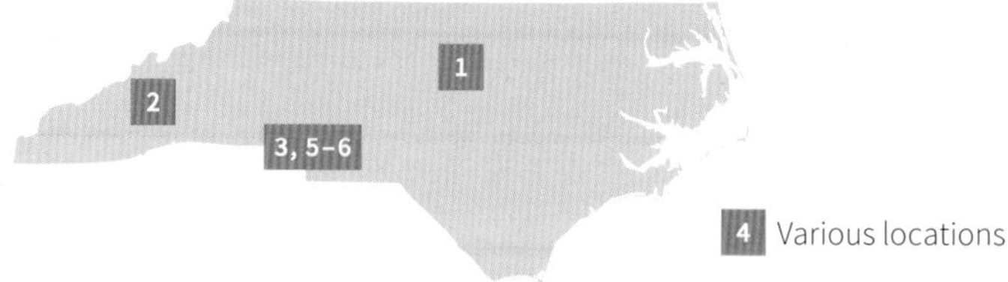

1 Ackland Art Museum at the University of North Carolina at Chapel Hill

101 S. Columbia St., Chapel Hill, NC 27514; 919-966-5736
ackland.org

The permanent collection contains about 17,000 artworks, including North Carolina pottery, African art, European and American art from 1600 to 1900, modern and contemporary works, North Carolina's leading collection of Asian art, and more. Closed Monday–Tuesday, January 1, July 4, Thanksgiving, and December 24–25. Free admission.

2 Asheville Art Museum

2 S. Pack Square, Asheville, NC 28801; 828-253-3227
ashevilleart.org

The Asheville Art Museum celebrated its 70th anniversary in 2018 and underwent a complete remodel. The museum now has a new glass entrance, expanded exhibition and gallery space, and a rooftop sculpture terrace with a café, along with studios and classrooms. The collection includes more than 8,000 works of 20th- and 21st-century American art. Closed Monday, January 1, July 4, Thanksgiving, and December 24–25. Admission charged.

3 Bechtler Museum of Modern Art

420 S. Tryon St., Charlotte, NC 28202; 704-353-9200
bechtler.org

This museum opened January 2, 2010, and continues to delight visitors with its collection of works from some of the most influential artists of the mid-20th century: Max Ernst, Alberto Giacometti, Barbara Hepworth, Pablo Picasso, Andy Warhol, and others. Closed Tuesday, January 1, Thanksgiving, and December 25. Admission charged.

4 Benjamin F. Long IV Fresco Trail

Various locations
blueridgeheritage.com/destinations/blue-ridge-frescoes

North Carolina is fortunate to hold many of the treasures created by famed fresco painter Ben Long. He is one of the few artists who have mastered the art of painting on wet plaster—it's the same process Michelangelo used in his work at the Sistine Chapel. The Benjamin F. Long IV Fresco Trail is comprised of nine frescoes in six locations in the Blue Ridge National Heritage Area in North Carolina. The locations include St. Mary's Episcopal Church (400 Beaver Creek School Road, West Jefferson, NC 28694; 336-982-3076; phc.diocesewnc.org/4stmarys.html); Holy Trinity Episcopal Church (195 J.W. Luke Road, West Jefferson, NC 28694; 336-982-3076; phc.diocesewnc.org/3holytrinity.html); Chapel of the Prodigal, Montreat College (310 Gaither Cir., Montreat, NC 28757; 828-669-8012, ext. 3820; montreat.edu); City of Morganton Municipal Auditorium (401 S. College St., Morganton, NC 28655; 828-438-5294; commaonline.org); E.H. Sloop Chapel, Crossnore School (100 DAR Dr., Crossnore, NC 28616; 828-733-4305; crossnore.org); and St. Paul's Episcopal Church (206 W. Cowles St., Wilkesboro, NC 28697; 336-667-4231; stpaulwilkesboro.org). Hours vary by location. Free admission; donations appreciated.

5 Harvey B. Gantt Center for African-American Arts + Culture

551 S. Tryon St., Charlotte, NC 28202; 704-547-3700
ganttcenter.org

Showcasing African-American art, history, and culture, this 46,500-square-foot center is named after Charlotte's first black mayor, Harvey B. Gantt, who served two terms. The John and Vivian Hewitt Collection of African-American Art, part of the center's permanent collection, features the works of Romare Bearden, Elizabeth Catlett, Ann Tanksley, Henry Ossawa Tanner, and others. Closed Monday, January 1, Easter, Memorial Day, July 4, Labor Day, Thanksgiving, and December 25. Admission charged.

6 Mint Museum

500 S. Tryon St., Charlotte, NC 28202; 704-337-2000
2730 Randolph Road, Charlotte, NC 28207; 704-337-2000
mintmuseum.org

The Randolph location houses ceramics and decorative art, as well as art from Europe, Africa, and the ancient Americas. The Uptown location houses the Craft + Design collection, which focuses on contemporary decorative arts in glass, fiber art, metal, studio jewelry, design, furniture, wood art, and clay. In addition, Uptown has collections of American, European, and contemporary art. Closed Monday, Tuesday, Easter, Memorial Day, July 4, Labor Day, Thanksgiving, and December 24–25. Admission charged.

7 Nasher Museum of Art at Duke University

2001 Campus Dr., Durham, NC 27705; 919-684-5135
nasher.duke.edu

Opened in 2005, the museum has focused on developing an incredible collection of contemporary art, especially works created by African American artists including Amy Sherald, Barkley L. Hendricks, and others. Café on-site. Closed Monday, January 1, July 4, Thanksgiving, and December 24–25. Admission charged; free admission on Thursday.

8 North Carolina Museum of Art

2110 Blue Ridge Road, Raleigh, NC 27607; 919-839-6262
ncartmuseum.org

The North Carolina General Assembly approved spending $1 million in 1947 on art that makes up the permanent collection here. This move made North Carolina the first state in the country to use public funds to establish an art museum. The 164-acre Ann and Jim Goodnight Museum Park includes the East Building, West Building, amphitheater, and multiple outdoor art installations around the grounds. The permanent collection of the North Carolina Museum of Art includes 30 works by Auguste Rodin. Closed Monday, January 1, Thanksgiving, and December 24–25; the park is open daily year-round, dawn–dusk. Free admission to the permanent collection and the park; admission charged for the West Building, some special exhibits, and some events.

9 Reynolda House Museum of American Art

2250 Reynolda Road, Winston-Salem, NC 27106; 888-663-1149
reynoldahouse.org

This museum is located in the former home of R. J. and Katharine Reynolds. R. J. accumulated his wealth as founder of the R. J. Reynolds Tobacco Company. A 200-piece collection of American art features artists such as Georgia O'Keeffe, Grant Wood, Frederic Church, Gilbert Stuart, Albert Bierstadt, and more. In addition to paintings and sculptures, the museum's collections of decorative arts, furnishings, costumes, and vintage toys delight guests. Closed Monday, the month of January, Thanksgiving, and December 24–25. Admission charged, but free to members, children age 18 and under, students or military personnel with ID, and employees of Wake Forest University and Wake Forest Baptist Medical Center.

10 Weatherspoon Art Museum

500 Tate St., Greensboro, NC 27403; 336-334-5770
weatherspoon.uncg.edu

This museum holds almost 6,000 pieces of art in its permanent collection, which contains the collection of sisters Claribel and Etta Cone, featuring works of Henri Matisse and Pablo Picasso among others. The museum is also proud of its Lenoir C. Wright Collection of Japanese woodblock prints. Closed Monday, January 1, Good Friday, July 4, Thanksgiving, day after Thanksgiving, and December 24–31. Free admission and parking.

Explore the 8,000-acre estate and the 179,000-square-foot home at Biltmore Estate.

DON'T FALL VICTIM to a misconception about Biltmore Estate. Some people think they can fit a visit to George Vanderbilt's castle into a day trip to Asheville, but Biltmore is a day trip in itself. You'll wind up disappointed if you think you can pop in and out in 2–3 hours. Ideally, plan to extend the trip over two days so you can fully enjoy what the estate has to offer. Check biltmore.com before heading out—Biltmore offers discounts on tickets purchased online seven days before a visit. There's also a discount for next-day admission and for kids ages 10–16; plus kids age 9 and under are admitted free.

HISTORIC SITES & MUSEUMS:

Biltmore Estate

1 Biltmore Estate

1 Lodge St., Asheville, NC 28803; 800-411-3812
biltmore.com
Open daily, year-round. Admission charged.

During a stay at the original Battery Park Hotel in downtown Asheville in the late 1800s, George Washington Vanderbilt gazed out at the stunning Blue Ridge Mountains of Western North Carolina and knew he had found the location for a fabulous mansion. He quickly scooped up 125,000 acres and hired some of the world's top artisans to make his elaborate dream a reality. It took workers six years to construct the 250-room palace, which remains America's largest privately owned home. Vanderbilt opened the doors to family and friends on December 24, 1895—they oohed and aahed at his lavish decor, as well as rare amenities for the time: electricity, central heating, and running water. George and his wife, Edith, raised their only child, Cornelia, in the opulent house, filled with 16th-century tapestries and priceless treasures from around the globe. After George died in 1914 at the age of 51, Edith sold 87,000 acres of the estate to the federal government for formation of the Pisgah National Forest. Cornelia inherited the house and married the Honorable John Francis Amherst Cecil (pronounced Sess-ul) on April 29, 1924. In 1930 the Cecils decided to open the house for public tours as a way to help the local economy by increasing tourism during the Great Depression. They had two sons: William A. V. Cecil and George Cecil. William's children, Bill Cecil and Dini Cecil Pickering, are at the helm of this thriving family business today.

2 The Gardens

Vanderbilt hired Frederick Law Olmsted to create a landscaping plan for the estate, which includes formal and informal gardens. Known as America's foremost landscape architect, Olmsted produced an expert vision for land management at Biltmore. For the Approach Road, Olmsted focused on native plants. He added 10,000 rhododendrons, as well as mountain laurels and other plants, to the road to the house. While the landscape is plush and manicured today, it needed to be tamed when Olmsted first sized up the property. He described the "barrenness and the miserable character of its woods" in a letter to a friend. Today the grounds and gardens are revered for their beauty. Spring is a particularly beautiful time at Biltmore, with thousands of tulips, dogwoods, redbuds, azaleas, and forsythia, all bursting with color. In late summer, the focus turns to the roses and perennials, and in fall, the vibrant chrysanthemums and salvias mix with the turning of the leaves.

3 The Hotels

For many years, guests at Biltmore Estate would remark how wonderful it would be to stay overnight there. While guest rooms aren't offered in Vanderbilt's house, lodging is available on the grounds. The Inn at Biltmore Estate opened in 2001, giving guests a taste of luxurious accommodations and opportunities to book appointments in its full-service spa. It lies on a hill above Antler Hill Village and the winery. In 2015 the 209-room Village Hotel opened in Antler Hill Village. And if you want something a little more private, Biltmore offers a two-bedroom, two-bath cottage. Check biltmore.com/stay/cottage for availability.

4 The House

Famed architect Richard Morris Hunt designed the 175,000-square-foot, 250-room home. It has four levels, 35 guest and family rooms, 45 bathrooms, 65 fireplaces, a library containing more than 10,000 volumes (the house has more than 23,000 in all), an indoor swimming pool and bowling alley, 3 kitchens, and 3 laundry rooms. It was named a National Historic Landmark in 1963. There are several options for touring the house. A self-guided tour allows visitors to go at their own pace as they move from room to room and investigate the priceless treasures. Add-ons include an audio guide, as well as guided tours led by knowledgeable staff who can relate more personal stories about the Vanderbilts and their glamorous lifestyle and parties. Plan on spending at least 2 hours touring the home, and leave time to have a relaxing meal, explore the gardens, and tour Antler Hill Village with the winery, shops, and additional places to eat. Behind-the-scenes guided tours at the house include a rooftop tour, a premium 2-hour tour with a personal guide, and a Legacy of the Land tour. During the holiday season, Candlelight Christmas Evenings showcase a choir accompanied by live music. All of the additional tours require an extra fee added to the general admission price.

5 Outdoor Experiences

While I don't advise skipping a house tour (it is magnificent) if you've never seen it before, there are so many outdoor activities available at Biltmore that you could plan a day trip at the estate and enjoy its offerings without ever stepping inside a building. The opportunities here include hiking, horseback riding, fly-fishing, falconry, river float trips on the French Broad River (which runs through the property), carriage rides, Segway tours, sporting clay shooting and lessons, and off-road experiences in a Land Rover. Biltmore also hosts an annual marathon and half-marathon on the estate and other outdoor-related events throughout the year.

6 The Restaurants

Vanderbilt created Biltmore to be self-sufficient. As a result of that vision, Biltmore raises its own livestock, free from growth hormones and antibiotics, and also plants and harvests a variety of vegetables, fresh herbs, seasonal fruits and berries, and other items. Restaurants on the estate use much of what is raised, but when demand exceeds production, Biltmore works with area farmers and food producers to source local ingredients and meats. Dining options are scattered across the estate. The Stable Café, located next to the house, is a family favorite. It's housed in the former horse stable and serves up estate-raised Angus beef, rotisserie chicken, soups, salads, and more. A courtyard adjacent to the house includes a bakeshop, ice cream parlor, the Conservatory Café, and Courtyard Market. Deerpark Restaurant, located in a converted dairy barn, serves diners buffet-style. At Antler Hill Village, the restaurants include The Bistro and Cedric's Tavern, along with the Smokehouse (Carolina barbecue) and the Creamery (ice cream, pastries, and gourmet coffees). Plus, there are restaurants at The Inn on Biltmore Estate: The Dining Room, which offers upscale dining as well as afternoon tea, and the Library Lounge. At the Village Hotel, there's the Village Social restaurant and The Kitchen, which offers grab-and-go items.

7 The Shops

The grandeur of the Vanderbilts' home might inspire you to purchase some objects reflective of their style. There are quite a few shops here, starting with the Gate House Shop at the main entrance. There are also shops adjacent to the house, on the lower level of the Conservatory, at Antler Hill Village, and in the hotels. The merchandise covers everything from Biltmore wine and jewelry to books and candy to home decor and gardening supplies.

8 The Winery

Located in Antler Hill Village, the Biltmore Winery features the estate's handcrafted vintages. Visitors can enjoy complimentary samples of an assortment of reds, whites, and rosés in the tasting room. Pick up bottles for purchase in the lavish shop, filled with gourmet food items, kitchen accessories, and Biltmore memorabilia. Also offered are a Behind-the-Scenes Winery Tour and specialty wine experiences, such as the Red Wine & Chocolate Tasting (for an additional fee). William Cecil began planting the Biltmore Vineyards in the early 1970s. He traveled to France, where he hired Philippe Jourdain, a sixth-generation winemaker, to become the estate's first winemaker. Biltmore bottled its first wines in 1984. Today, Biltmore produces approximately 150,000 cases of its award-winning wines each year. The Biltmore Winery holds the distinction as the country's most visited winery.

Unto These Hills, an outdoor drama in Cherokee, debuted on July 1, 1950, and remains popular today. (courtesy of the Cherokee Historical Association)

CHEROKEE HISTORY is interwoven with the western part of the state, and it's a story embedded with pain and sorrow due to the forced removal of many Cherokee who traveled the Trail of Tears. Spend time outdoors connecting with the land; experience Cherokee life in a living-history village; watch a long-running outdoor drama telling the Cherokees' story; and explore the rich heritage of Cherokee arts, crafts, music, dance, and storytelling.

HISTORIC SITES & MUSEUMS: Cherokee Indian Culture

1 Cherokee Voices Festival

589 Tsali Blvd., Cherokee, NC 28719; 828-497-3481, ext. 306
visitcherokeenc.com/events/detail/cherokee-voices-festival or cherokeemuseum.org

Held at the Museum of the Cherokee Indian in June, this annual free festival presents Cherokee heritage and culture through traditional dance and music, arts and crafts, storytelling, and other events.

2 Fire Mountain Trails

218 Drama Road, Cherokee, NC 28719
visitcherokeenc.com/itinerary-builder/poi/fire_mountain_trails

After exploring the Oconaluftee Indian Village, spend time enjoying a 10.5-mile network of trails known as the Fire Mountain Trails. The trailhead is only 100 yards or so from the village. The trails are perfect for mountain biking, hiking, and running. They're open 24-7.

3 Harrah's Cherokee Casino Resort

777 Casino Dr., Cherokee, NC 28719; 828-497-7777
caesars.com/harrahs-cherokee

Another way to claim cash in Cherokee is to try your hand at the games at Harrah's Cherokee Casino. It's owned by the Eastern Band of Cherokee Indians and first opened in 1997 offering video poker and slot machines. The tribe successfully lobbied the state of North Carolina to allow them to add live dice and card games in 2012. The resort complex includes more than 1,100 hotel rooms, a variety of bars and restaurants (including Chefs Stage Buffet and Ruth's Chris Steak House), an indoor pool, an outdoor pool, a 24-7 fitness room, and UltraStar Multi-tainment Center with bowling and arcade games, plus a 3,000-seat event center for concerts and other events.

4 Museum of the Cherokee Indian

589 Tsali Blvd., Cherokee, NC 28719; 828-497-3481
cherokeemuseum.org

This museum covers 13,000 years of Cherokee history. It's filled with priceless artifacts, computer-generated animation and other special

A 22-foot-tall wooden sculpture of Sequoyah by artist Peter Toth greets visitors at the Museum of the Cherokee Indian.
(courtesy of the Museum of the Cherokee Indian)

effects, art, and life-size figures. The holdings include thousands of photographs dating from the 1880s, 4,000 books, materials written in the Cherokee language, and more. An Education and Research Wing allows museum members and scholars to engage in research by appointment. There's also a digital library online. Closed January 1 and December 25. The museum charges admission but hosts a free Cherokee Heritage Day on one Saturday each month. This family-friendly event includes hands-on craft workshops and demonstrations, storytelling, dancing, and more.

5 Oconaluftee Indian Village

778 Drama Road, Cherokee, NC 28719; 828-497-2111
cherokeehistorical.org/oconaluftee-indian-village

This unique site gives visitors a closer look at the life of Cherokee Indians in North Carolina. Guided tours introduce participants to Cherokee artists who demonstrate different crafts: basketry, pottery, weaponry, finger weaving, and more. Explore replicas of Cherokee homes and interact with costumed reenactors in the living-history area, or hear lectures on Cherokee culture and history. Daily programs include traditional dance shows and Time of War reenactments. Plus, take time to enjoy a nature trail and browse the Eternal Flame Gift Shop. Open mid-April–mid-November; closed Sunday (also closed Mondays in April and late October–November). Admission charged.

6 Qualla Arts & Crafts Mutual

645 Tsali Blvd., Cherokee, NC 28719; 828-497-3103
quallaartsandcrafts.com

Established in 1946, Qualla Arts and Crafts currently highlights the talents of more than 250 members with a large assortment of handwoven baskets, carved items, pottery, beaded jewelry, and other objects. Closed January 1, Thanksgiving, and December 25. Free admission.

7 Trout Tournaments

828-359-6110
fishcherokee.com/events

Perhaps one of the best ways to experience Cherokee is to have a direct connection with nature. One popular way to find the zen of the moment is by casting a line into the water in hopes of snagging a trout. A permit is required to fish. Trout tournaments throughout the year provide opportunities for you to win cash by catching tagged fish. The Opening Day Fishing Tournament offers $20,000 in prizes. There's also a Memorial Day Trout Tournament, Tim Hill Memorial Trout Tournament (July), Qualla Country Trout Tournament (September), and a Rumble in the Rhododendron Fly-Fishing Tournament (a two-person team event held in November). Registration fees and permits are required for each tournament. Register online at fishcherokee.com.

8 *Unto These Hills* Outdoor Drama

688 Drama Road, Cherokee, NC 28719; 828-497-2111
cherokeehistorical.org/unto-these-hills

This qualifies as a night trip instead of a day trip, but it's still a worthy addition to your agenda. During its season (June–mid-August), shows occur at 8 p.m. Monday–Saturday. A preshow begins at 7:30 p.m. The drama depicts the history of the Cherokee Indians and takes place rain or shine in an open-air theater that seats more than 2,500 people. On stage, you'll witness drama, frustration, tragedy, dancing, and triumph. Free parking is available next to the

Day-trippers can interact with Cherokee craftspeople at the Oconaluftee Indian Village. (courtesy of the Cherokee Historical Association)

Oconaluftee Indian Village. Options for tickets include a combo pass that allows admittance into the show, Oconaluftee Indian Village, and the Museum of the Cherokee Indian.

Other Indian Tribes of North Carolina

Catawba Indian Nation
catawbaindian.net

Coharie Tribe
coharietribe.org

Haliwa-Saponi Indians
haliwa-saponi.com

Lumbee Tribe
lumbeetribe.com

Meherrin Nation
meherrinnation.org

Occaneechi Band of the Saponi Nation
obsn.org

Sappony Indians
sappony.org

Waccamaw Siouan Indians
waccamaw-siouan.net

Brinegar Cabin, built in the late 1800s, sits adjacent to the Blue Ridge Parkway.

AMID THE BEAUTIFUL SCENERY, a strong heritage runs through North Carolina's communities. It's important to take a look back and find out how certain traditions emerged and to remember the people who came before. North Carolina has many sites and museums to preserve the heritage of the state, from mountain homesteads to Civil War history to the civil rights movement.

HISTORIC SITES & MUSEUMS:
Heritage Sites

Explore 100 acres of gardens and 90 buildings at Old Salem Museums & Gardens.

1 Bennett Place

4409 Bennett Memorial Road, Durham, NC 27705; 919-383-4345
historicsites.nc.gov/all-sites/bennett-place

Bennett Place is a key Civil War site—where Confederate General Joseph Johnston negotiated the surrender of the Southern armies in North and South Carolina, Georgia, and Florida. This farmhouse was chosen because it was located between General Johnston's headquarters in Greensboro and Union General William T. Sherman's headquarters in Raleigh. Bennett farm has been fully restored to look like it did when the generals met here in 1865. A visitor center contains exhibits, artifacts, and a gift shop. The outside area includes the Unity Monument, outdoor exhibits, walking trails, and picnic areas. Closed Sunday, Monday, January 1, Good Friday, July 4, Veterans Day, Thanksgiving, day after Thanksgiving, and December 24–26. Free admission; donations appreciated.

2 Brinegar Cabin

Milepost 238.5 on the Blue Ridge Pkwy., Traphill, NC 28685; 828-348-3400
nps.gov/articles/550138.htm

In the late 1800s, Martin Brinegar and his wife, Caroline, bought land where they raised livestock and tended crops. Today, visitors can glimpse a bit of what their homestead was like. The National Park Service restored the Brinegar Cabin as an interpretive exhibit at milepost 238.5 on the Blue Ridge Parkway; in 1972 it was listed on the National Register of Historic Places. The 2.5-acre site includes the cabin and three other structures: a granary, a springhouse, and an outhouse, plus an interpretive garden. During the summer months, interpreters are on hand at select times for craft demonstrations, such as spinning yarn. Plus, the annual Brinegar Day in September demonstrates what life was like for the Brinegars. Open Memorial Day weekend to early November, Saturday–Sunday. Free admission.

3 Charlotte Hawkins Brown Museum

6136 Burlington Road, Gibsonville, NC 27249: 336-449-4846
historicsites.nc.gov/all-sites/charlotte-hawkins-brown-museum

Dr. Charlotte Hawkins Brown founded the Palmer Memorial Institute in 1902 as a school for African American students. Today, visitors can explore the restored campus buildings for a unique learning experience. Existing structures include Brown's personal home (Canary Cottage), the Carrie M. Stone Teacher's Cottage (housing for unmarried female teachers), Charles W. Eliot Hall (boys' dorm), Brown's grave site and meditation altar, Kimball Hall (formerly the school dining hall), Galen L. Stone Hall (girls' dorm), the Massachusetts Congregational Women's Cottage (girls' home economics practice house), and The Tea House (canteen, bookstore, and hands-on learning center for business management). Closed Sunday, Monday, January 1, Good Friday, July 4, Veterans Day, Thanksgiving, day after Thanksgiving, and December 24–26. Free admission; donations appreciated.

4 Cradle of Forestry in America

11250 Pisgah Hwy., Pisgah Forest, NC 28768; 828-877-3130
cradleofforestry.com

The Cradle of Forestry, tied to George Vanderbilt's forestry initiatives at Biltmore Estate, celebrates the birthplace of science-based forest management in America. Congress created this 6,500-acre heritage site in 1968 to "preserve, develop, and make available to this and future generations the birthplace of forestry and forestry education in America." The entrance is located 4 miles from milepost 412 on the Blue Ridge Parkway. Walk paved interpretative trails to see where forestry students at the Biltmore Forest School trained and lived. The Forest Discovery Center has a gift shop and café. Special events are staged when the center is open. Open early April–November. Admission charged.

5 Fort Fisher

1610 Fort Fisher Blvd. S, Kure Beach, NC 28449; 910-251-7340
historicsites.nc.gov/all-sites/fort-fisher

Fort Fisher was an instrumental site during the Civil War but ultimately fell after a Federal amphibious assault on January 15, 1865. Less than 10% of the fort's earth fortification remains. The rest of the tour includes a visitor center, a gift shop, trails, outdoor exhibits, and monuments. Check the schedule for reenactments and costumed guided tours. Closed Monday, January 1, Good Friday, July 4, Veterans Day, Thanksgiving, day after Thanksgiving, and December 24–26. Free admission.

6 Hickory Ridge Living History Museum

591 Horn in the West Dr., Boone, NC 28607; 828-264-2120
hornin thewest.com

Interpreters in period clothing lead visitors through an immersive experience to learn more about the daily lives of early mountain settlers from the late 18th century and about such events as the Revolutionary War. The museum has been in operation since 1980. The outdoor drama *Horn in the West,* about Daniel Boone and the Revolutionary War, takes place at the Daniel Boone Amphitheatre. Arrive early for a tour of the museum before the show; it opens at 5:30 p.m. on show nights. Open April–late November, Tuesday–Saturday, limited hours. Show runs late June–early August, Tuesday–Sunday. Admission charged; show tickets cost an additional fee.

7 Historic Bath

207 Carteret St., Bath, NC 27808; 252-923-3971
historicsites.nc.gov/all-sites/historic-bath

Bath claims the distinction of being the first incorporated town and first port in North Carolina. Tours are offered of some of the oldest homes in town: Palmer-Marsh House (circa 1751), Bonner House (circa 1835), and Van Der Veer House (circa 1790). Another notable history tidbit: Bath was the home of Blackbeard the Pirate. Closed Sunday, Monday, January 1, Good Friday, July 4, Veterans Day, Thanksgiving, day after Thanksgiving, and December 24–2. Admission charged.

8 Horne Creek Living Historical Farm

308 Horne Creek Farm Road, Pinnacle, NC 27043; 336-325-2298
historicsites.nc.gov/all-sites/horne-creek-farm

Go back in time and experience what life was like in the early 1900s when the Hauser family lived on this site. Visitors can explore the family's farmhouse, tobacco-curing barn, corncrib, heritage apple orchard, and more. A handicapped-accessible visitor center, walking trails, a gift shop, and picnic tables round out the historical site. Closed Sunday, Monday, January 1, Good Friday, July 4, Veterans Day, Thanksgiving, day after Thanksgiving, and December 24–26. Free admission; donations appreciated.

9 International Civil Rights Center & Museum

134 S. Elm St., Greensboro, NC 27401; 336-274-9199
sitinmovement.org

On February 1, 1960, four young black men—all students at the Agricultural and Mechanical College for the Colored Race (now known as the North Carolina Agricultural and Technical State University)—staged a sit-in at the segregated Woolworth's lunch counter in Greensboro. They refused to leave after being denied service, and their nonviolent civil rights protest spread to other towns. Their actions forced Woolworth's and other businesses to change their policies about whom they would serve. The museum includes the original lunch counter and stools where the Greensboro Four began their protest, as well as pictures, artifacts, videos, and interactive components to tell the story of the American civil rights movement. Closed Sunday. Admission charged.

10 Mountain Gateway Museum and Heritage Center

24 Water St., Old Fort, NC 28762; 828-668-9259
mgmnc.org

Explore Southern Appalachian culture through exhibits and information about folk medicine, spinning, weaving, traditional crafts, moonshining, and agricultural topics. The campus includes a main building constructed in 1936 and two cabins, the Morgan Cabin and the Stepp Cabin. Closed Monday, January 1, Good Friday, July 4, Veterans Day, Thanksgiving, day after Thanksgiving, and December 24–26. Free admission; donations appreciated. Admission charged for some programs and exhibits.

11 Mount Airy Museum of Regional History

301 N. Main St., Mount Airy, NC 27030; 336-786-4478
northcarolinamuseum.org

Encompassing four floors of history with almost 35,000 square feet of permanent exhibit space, the Mount Airy Museum of Regional History provides opportunities for learning about regional American Indians and early settlers, listening to the region's unique old-time music, finding out about the largest open-face granite quarry in the world, and "meeting" famous people who hailed from Mount Airy: Andy Griffith, singer Donna Fargo, musician Tommy Jarrell, and Siamese American conjoined twins Chang and Eng Bunker. The third floor holds a hands-on history gallery for children. Closed Sunday, Monday, Thanksgiving, and December 25. Admission charged.

12 Old Salem Museums & Gardens

900 Old Salem Road, Winston-Salem, NC 27101; 336-721-7300
oldsalem.org

From furniture to decorative arts to weapons to musical instruments, maps, ceramics, and textiles, the Old Salem Collection is a comprehensive accumulation of objects from the Moravian town of Salem and the surrounding area. There are 90 buildings, and about a dozen of them—including a variety of houses, a fire engine house, a potter's workshop, a gunsmith shop, and a boys' school—are interpreted. In addition, take time to enjoy more than 100 acres of gardens and hands-on demonstrations. Many of the buildings are wheelchair accessible, plus there are exploration boxes for those with sensory issues. Closed Monday, January 1, Easter, Thanksgiving, and December 24–25. An all-in-one ticket, the best value, allows admission to the historic buildings and the Museum of Early Southern Decorative Arts (MESDA) self-guided galleries; these tickets are valid for two consecutive days. Two-shop tickets are also available.

13 Quilt Trails

Various locations in Western North Carolina; 828-682-7331
quilttrailswnc.org

Follow the colorful trail of quilt squares to learn more about the history of the region. You'll find a large concentration of the blocks in Mitchell and Yancey Counties—more than 200 colorful blocks on a variety of barns and other structures. Great effort is made to ensure that each block is unique. Download free maps online, and also check out the block list to pinpoint specific quilt blocks you want to see. The quilt trail movement began in 2001 when Donna Sue Groves launched the Ohio Quilt Barn Project; there are now quilt trails all over the country: barnquiltinfo.com.

14 Rural Heritage Museum

Mars Hill University, 80 Cascade St., Mars Hill, NC 28754; 828-689-1650
mhu.edu/about/what-to-do-and-see/museum

The permanent collection here includes objects once used by Appalachian homesteaders, such as spinning wheels, looms, farm tools, and other items that have been donated or purchased to showcase the region's heritage. Closed Monday, January 1, Good Friday, Easter, Thanksgiving, and December 25. Free admission.

15 Transylvania Heritage Museum

189 W. Main St., Brevard, NC 28712; 828-884-2347
transylvaniaheritage.org

Housed in a former home built in the 1890s, the museum originally stood on Main Street, but it was moved to 189 W. Main St. in the 1980s. Permanent holdings include heirlooms, artifacts, genealogical exhibits, photographs, and other items focusing on the history of Transylvania County. The exhibits are rotated twice a year. Open March–mid-December, Wednesday–Saturday; closed Good Friday, Easter, and Thanksgiving. Free admission; donations appreciated. The museum also runs the Second Floor House Museum at Silvermont at 364 E. Main St. (open March–October, Friday afternoon only), which also offers free admission.

16 Zebulon B. Vance Birthplace

911 Reems Creek Road, Weaverville, NC 28787; 828-645-6706
historicsites.nc.gov/all-sites/zebulon-b-vance-birthplace

Visit this pioneer farmstead located in Weaverville, just north of Asheville. It was the home of Zebulon B. Vance, a Civil War governor and post–Reconstruction senator. The site contains a two-story log cabin, an original slave cabin from the 1790s, and five outbuildings. Closed Sunday, Monday, January 1, Good Friday, July 4, Veterans Day, Thanksgiving, day after Thanksgiving, and December 24–26. Free admission; donations appreciated.

Tryon Palace, North Carolina's first permanent capitol

TIME TRAVEL MIGHT BE FICTION, but you may feel like a time traveler when you step inside homes that have been standing for decades. You'll be able to imagine what life was like when former residents lived in these houses—some have original furnishings and expert guides to paint a picture of the people who once lived there and what their lives were like.

HISTORIC SITES & MUSEUMS:

Historic Homes

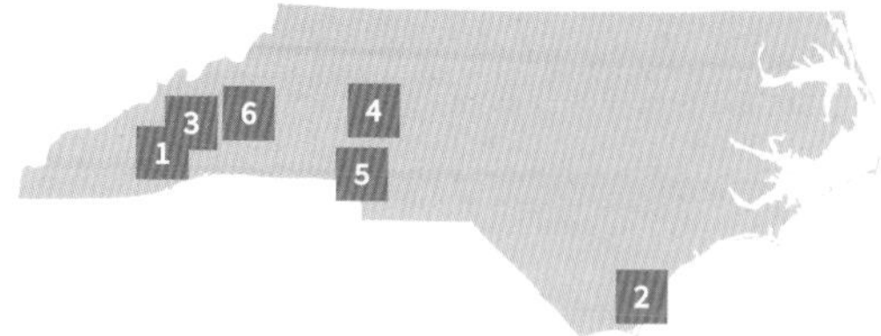

1 Allison-Deaver House

2753 Asheville Hwy., Pisgah Forest, NC 28768; 828-884-5137
tchistoricalsociety.com/?page_id=9

Log cabins were common in Western North Carolina in the early 1800s, but Benjamin Allison decided to build a two-story frame house for his family in 1815. He sold it in 1830 to William Deaver, who doubled the home by 1840. Open June–late October, Saturday–Sunday, and by appointment.

2 Bellamy Mansion Museum of History & Design Arts

503 Market St., Wilmington, NC 28401; 910-251-3700
bellamymansion.org

In 1972 the Bellamy Mansion became the target of arsonists, though firefighters were able to save much of the exterior. An extensive renovation of the interior took place in the 1990s, and it was ready to welcome guests in 1994 as the Bellamy Mansion Museum of History & Design Arts. Guided tours are available daily and begin on the hour, with the last tour starting at 4 p.m.; closed Thanksgiving and December 24–early January. Admission charged.

3 Biltmore House

1 Lodge St., Asheville, NC 28803; 800-411-3812
biltmore.com

Biltmore has its own chapter in this book (see page 44), but I would be remiss if I did not include it in the historic homes category. It took more than five years to complete George Vanderbilt's massive mansion. He hired some of the world's top artisans to use their talents in the design and construction. Today, the 250-room Biltmore House remains America's largest privately owned residence and welcomes more than a million visitors a year. Open daily, year-round. Admission charged.

4 Darshana Hall Plantation

235 Triplett Road, Cleveland, NC 27103; 704-872-3608
darshanahallplantation.com

Pioneer John McElwrath built the first home on this property in 1753. A Federal-style home followed in 1818. The Chambers family enlarged the cotton plantation from 4,000 to 12,000 acres. After 1903, it went through multiple owners until Harry Gatton took on the task of restoring the place in the 1950s. He sold it in 1969 to Dr. Meredith Hall, who named it Darshana, a Hindu term. Tours available by reservation; admission charged.

5 Duke Mansion

400 Hermitage Road, Charlotte, NC 28207; 704-714-4400
dukemansion.com

Built in 1915 in the Myers Park neighborhood (new at the time), this house is a remarkable specimen of Colonial Revival architecture. Its most famous owner was James Buchanan Duke, a tobacco and electric power industrialist. Today, the Duke Mansion, listed on the National Register of Historic Places and operated as a nonprofit, offers 20 guest rooms for overnight accommodations. It's fully accessible, with a ramp and elevator to upper floors. Book the whole house for a private house party or family reunion.

6 Historic Carson House

1805 US 70 W, Marion, NC 28752; 828-724-4948
historiccarsonhouse.com

This is one of those historic places where you wish the walls could talk. Built in the late 1700s, this two-story house served as the residence of the Carson family through the Revolutionary War, Civil War, North Carolina gold rush, and other historical moments. It also holds valuable information for researchers and those seeking clues to their family histories in the Mary M. Greenlee Genealogical Research and History Room. The house is open for tours April–November, Wednesday–Saturday (last tour begins at 3 p.m.) and Sunday (last tour at 4 p.m.), and by appointment; closed Easter, Mother's Day, Thanksgiving, and day after Thanksgiving. Admission charged.

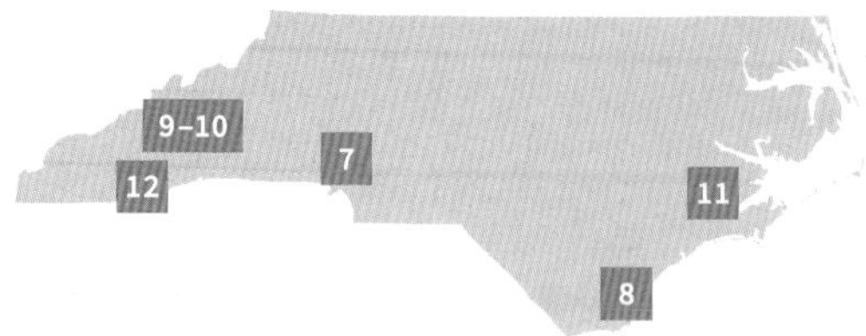

7 Historic Latta Plantation

5225 Sample Road, Huntersville, NC 28078; 704-875-2312
lattaplantation.org

This living-history farm is situated within the 1,343-acre Latta Nature Preserve. Visitors can get a peek of what life was like on this 19th-century cotton plantation with tours of the plantation home and 11 outbuildings. Special events, including reenactments, are held throughout the year. Closed Monday, January 1, Easter, Memorial Day, July 4, Labor Day, Thanksgiving, December 24–25, and December 31. Admission charged.

8 Poplar Grove Plantation

10200 US 17 N, Wilmington, NC 28411; 910-686-9518
poplargrove.org

In its day, this plantation cultivated sweet potatoes and peanuts. It stayed in the Foy family for six generations, from 1795 to 1971. In 1980 the home, which is listed on the National Register of Historic Places, was restored and opened as a museum. Tours offered March–October, Monday–Saturday (June–August, last tour at 3:30 p.m.; otherwise, last tour at 2:30 p.m.), and November–February, Saturday only (last tour at 2:30 p.m.). Admission charged.

9 Reynolds Mansion Bed & Breakfast Inn

100 Reynolds Heights, Asheville, NC 28804; 828-258-1111
thereynoldsmansion.com

This house is one of fewer than 10 pre–Civil War brick houses still in existence in Western North Carolina. Farmer Daniel Reynolds built it in 1847, and a succession of family members lived in the house, including Senator Robert Rice Reynolds and his daughter, Mamie, who teethed on the famed Hope Diamond and played with it in her sandbox. The famed necklace belonged to her grandmother, Evalyn Walsh McLean, who purchased the so-called cursed stone in 1911 from Cartier. The Hope Diamond is now in the permanent collection of the Smithsonian National Museum of Natural History in Washington, D.C. As for the home, it has been beautifully restored as a bed-and-breakfast owned by Billy Sanders and his partner, Michael Griffith.

10 Smith-McDowell House Museum

283 Victoria Road, Asheville, NC 28801; 828-253-9231
wnchistory.org/smith-mcdowell-house

When it was built in 1840, the home was known as the Buck House. The pre–Civil War building is noted as Asheville's oldest surviving house, as well as the oldest brick structure in Buncombe County, and it's listed on the National Register of Historic Places. Tours are offered Wednesday–Saturday; closed January 1, Easter, July 4, Thanksgiving, December 24–26, and December 31. Admission charged.

11 Tryon Palace

529 S. Front St., New Bern, NC 28562; 800-767-1560
tryonpalace.org

Built in 1770, Tryon Palace became the state's first permanent capitol and home to Royal Governor William Tryon and his family. Carve out at least a half-day to explore the offerings here, which include the Governor's Palace, historical homes, gardens, and galleries in the North Carolina History Center. Closed Monday, January 1, and December 24–26. Admission charged; choose a One-Day Pass to explore everything. If you want to focus on specific activities, you can choose to buy a Galleries Pass or a Gardens Pass.

12 Zachary-Tolbert House

1940 NC 107 S, Cashiers, NC 28717; 828-743-7710
blueridgeheritage.com/destinations/zachary-tolbert-house or cashiershistoricalsociety.org

Imagine receiving a house as a wedding present. That's what happened in 1852 when Mordecai Zachary presented it to his bride, Elvira Keener. He had begun building it 10 years earlier. They had a happy life there, raising 12 children in the home. The structure later served as the summer home for three different families. Tours of the eight-room Greek Revival–style frame house are offered late May–late October, Friday–Saturday. Admission charged.

North Carolina Museum of Natural Sciences, the state's most visited museum

YOU ARE CERTAIN to make some new discoveries about North Carolina when you spend time in these remarkable museums. History doesn't have to be boring. Look a bit closer and you'll find fascinating stories, artifacts, and other information about the people and events from past years.

HISTORIC SITES & MUSEUMS:

History Museums

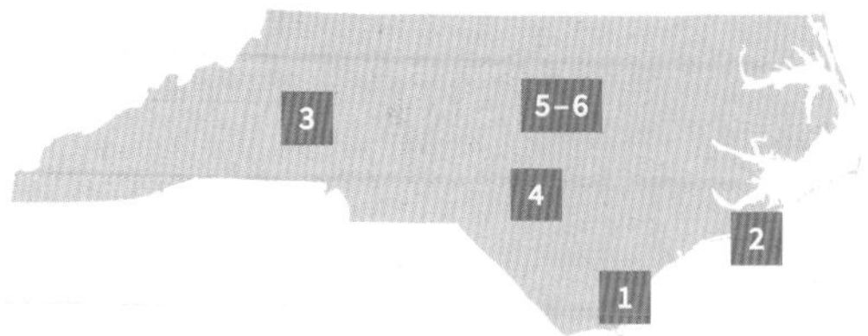

1 Cape Fear Museum of History and Science

814 Market St., Wilmington, NC 28401; 910-798-4370
capefearmuseum.com

The original mission of the museum, when it was founded in 1898, was to preserve Confederate objects and memories of the Civil War. Its focus is now much broader and encompasses the region's art, history, and science. Explore the museum's permanent and temporary exhibits or attend special events and programming. The ongoing hands-on exhibit titled *Michael Jordan Discovery Gallery* showcases the environment of the Lower Cape Fear area. Closed Mondays from Memorial Day to Labor Day, January 1, Thanksgiving, and December 24–25. Admission charged.

2 History Museum of Carteret County

1008 Arendell St., Morehead City, NC 28557; 252-247-7533
carterethistory.org

Period clothing and textiles, as well as custom furniture, glasswork, art, and military memorabilia, are on display here; the items represent the heritage of county residents. The museum also has more than 10,000 books in its Jack Goodwin Research Library and an extensive archive of photographs. The museum keeps a steady calendar of special events, seminars, and live music. Closed Saturday–Monday (open the first Saturday of each month), Thanksgiving, and December 24–25. Admission charged; free for age 5 and under.

3 History Museum of Catawba County

30 N. College Ave., Newton, NC 28658; 828-465-0383
catawbahistory.org

The collection includes objects such as tools and furniture from the region's early settlers. Visitors can walk through a 1920s medical office and see two full-scale antebellum parlors. Other highlights include a 1930s race car, firearms, flags, and military uniforms (including a British red coat from the Revolutionary War). Closed Sunday–Monday, January 1, July 4, Thanksgiving, day after Thanksgiving, and December 23–26. Free admission; donations appreciated.

4 Museum of the Cape Fear Historical Complex

801 Arsenal Ave., Fayetteville, NC 28305; 910-500-4240
museumofthecapefear.ncdcr.gov

This historical complex is comprised of a main museum building, the 1897 Poe House, and Arsenal Park (a former ordnance factory). Fayetteville businessman Edgar Allen Poe (not to be confused with the famed writer) married Josephine Montague in 1880, and they raised eight children in the home. You'll also find interactive programs, living-history programs, demonstrations, and exhibitions. Closed Monday, January 1, Easter, July 4, Thanksgiving, and December 24–25. Free admission.

5 North Carolina Museum of History

5 E. Edenton St., Raleigh, NC 27601; 919-814-7000
ncmuseumofhistory.org

The story of North Carolina is told through various exhibits, artifacts, and narratives in this Smithsonian affiliate. Free guided tours, as well as a few fee-based tours oriented to school groups, are available. Special events and festivals are held throughout the year. Closed January 1, Easter, Thanksgiving, and December 24–25. Free admission; some special exhibits require a fee.

6 North Carolina Museum of Natural Sciences

11 W. Jones St., Raleigh, NC 27601; 919-707-9800
naturalsciences.org

This downtown Raleigh facility includes the Nature Exploration Center and Nature Research Center (919-707-8080). There's so much to explore here that you will want to download the NC Museum of Natural Sciences app before your visit; the Museum Guide is also helpful and available to download from the website's Permanent Exhibitions page. Make new discoveries, attend special events, dine at the Daily Planet Cafe, and keep an eye out for special exhibitions. At a separate location at 1671 Gold Star Dr. in Raleigh, you can visit the Prairie Ridge Ecostation (919-707-8888), an outdoor learning space. Closed January 1, Thanksgiving, and December 24–25; Prairie Ridge is also closed Martin Luther King Jr. Day, Good Friday, Memorial Day, July 4, Labor Day, Veterans Day, day after Thanksgiving, and December 26. Free admission; donations appreciated.

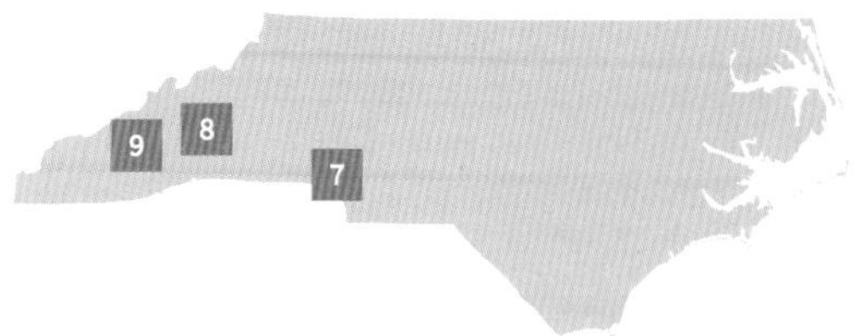

7 The Schiele Museum of Natural History

1500 E. Garrison Blvd., Gastonia, NC 28054; 704-866-6900
schielemuseum.org

This museum took shape in 1961 when Rudolph "Bud" Schiele worked out a plan with officials in Gastonia to display his collection of animal specimens. The Gaston County Museum of Natural History is now known as The Schiele Museum of Natural History. Explore the exhibit galleries, follow a short nature trail, or see a program at the planetarium and science theater. The 18th-Century Backcountry Farm and Catawba Indian Village are open seasonally. The museum also offers special programs and has a gift shop. Closed Easter, Thanksgiving, and December 24–25. Admission charged, plus a separate fee for the Planetarium & Science Theater. At press time, admission was free on the second Tuesday of every month, through 2019.

The Schiele Museum of Natural History also includes outdoor exhibits, such as this 18th-century backcountry farm.

8 Swannanoa Valley Museum & History Center

223 W. State St., Black Mountain, NC 28711; 828-669-9566
history.swannanoavalleymuseum.org

This place features history inside and out as it is housed in a 1921 firehouse designed by Richard Sharp Smith, who was the supervising architect at Biltmore House. The second floor contains a permanent exhibit on the history of the Swannanoa Valley, while the first floor transforms annually with temporary exhibitions. Special events include a hiking series that explores the region firsthand. Open mid-April–October, Tuesday–Saturday, and by appointment. Suggested donation of $5, but free to members, students, and youth under the age of 18.

9 World Methodist Museum

575 N. Lakeshore Dr., Lake Junaluska, NC 28745; 828-456-7242
methodistmuseum.com

Discover the history of Methodism in Lake Junaluska at the World Methodist Museum. It's known, according to its website, as "the world's largest archive for Methodist history and Wesleyan heritage." Browse the vast array of artifacts—including many linked to founder John Wesley—as well as exhibits and stories. Open March–October, Tuesday–Saturday, and November–February, Tuesday–Friday; closed January 1, July 4, Thanksgiving, and December 25. Free admission.

Try your hand at making your own pottery.

CREATIVITY FLOWS EASILY across North Carolina, as seen through the works of talented artists and craftspeople. From the mountains to the coast, there are many places to see pottery or handwoven textiles, plus chances to watch working artists in action. There are opportunities, even within the confines of a day trip, to learn some new techniques and produce a finished product to take home. Or explore area arts and crafts schools to get a taste of what they offer.

FOR THE YOUNG AT HEART:
Arts & Crafts

1 Biltmore Industries Tour

111 Grovewood Road, Asheville, NC 28804; 828-253-7651
grovewood.com/history-tours

This is another place touched by the wealth and interest of George and Edith Vanderbilt, owners of the Biltmore Estate. The Vanderbilts established Biltmore Industries in 1901 and brought in two main instructors—Eleanor Vance and Charlotte Yale—to train students in woodworking and the production of fine wool cloth. Three years after George Vanderbilt died in 1914, Edith sold the operation to Fred Seely, son-in-law of Edwin Grove, who created the Grove Park Inn. Seely constructed seven buildings adjacent to the Grove Park Inn that included woodworking shops and facilities for Biltmore Industries. He named the buildings the Biltmore Homespun Shops. The Biltmore Industries Homespun Museum is next door to Grovewood Gallery. Guided tours are available on a first-come, first-serve basis April–November, Wednesday–Saturday, 1 p.m. Closed January–March, Thanksgiving, and December 25. Free admission; donations appreciated.

2 Black Mountain College Museum + Arts Center

120 College St., Asheville, NC 28801; 828-350-8484
blackmountaincollege.org

Black Mountain College operated for only 24 years, but some of the most influential artists of the time taught and studied there, including Josef and Anni Albers, Willem and Elaine de Kooning, Robert Rauschenberg, Franz Kline, Ruth Asawa, and others. Though the college was located in Black Mountain, this museum is in downtown Asheville. It features exhibitions, publications, and programs about this experimental college and its influence in the world of art, dance, theater, music, and performance. Closed Sunday, Tuesday, January 1, Martin Luther King Jr. Day, Presidents' Day, Memorial Day, July 4, Labor Day, Columbus Day, Veterans Day, Thanksgiving, and December 25. Free admission; donations suggested.

3 Folk Art Center

382 Blue Ridge Pkwy., Asheville, NC 28805; 828-523-4110
southernhighlandguild.org/folk-art-center

The Folk Art Center, home to the Southern Highland Craft Guild, offers three galleries and a library, as well as the guild's oldest craft store. (You can also access the Mountains-to-Sea Trail from the parking lot.) Artists demonstrate their crafts daily March–December, and special events are held throughout the year. The permanent collection includes about 250 pieces highlighting the best of Southern Appalachian woodworking, textiles, basketry, pottery, furniture, and more. Closed January 1, Thanksgiving, and December 25. Free admission.

4 John C. Campbell Folk School

1 Folk School Road, Brasstown, NC 28902; 828-837-2775
folkschool.org

Head to Brasstown for a fun day trip exploring a storied craft school. Tour the campus, peek in on some classes, explore the nature trails (the school sits on 300 acres), visit the craft shop, and even have a meal in the dining hall (reservations required), where the food is served family style. The experience may prompt you to scan the school's course offerings for future workshops to take. The full course catalog is available online. Classes cover a wide range of topics, from basketry to broom making to knitting, banjo lessons, blacksmithing, and so much more. There are weeklong offerings, as well as instruction held over a weekend. Grounds open daily, dawn–dusk; office open Monday–Friday; closed Thanksgiving and December 25. Free to look around; fees for courses.

5 Museum of North Carolina Handicrafts

49 Shelton St., Waynesville, NC 28786; 828-452-1551
sheltonhouse.org/museum

The museum, founded in 1977, preserves traditional crafts at the two-story historical Shelton House and displays antique farm equipment at the barn. Highlighted items in the house include a hand-turned chair by master chair maker Max Woody, pottery by Ben Owen, 19th-century cabinets built by local craftsmen, and a three-plank harvest table built circa 1845 by Levi Caldwell, plus quilts, Cherokee crafts, and items from the Civil War, World War II, and the Spanish American War. Closed November–March; closed Sunday–Monday the rest of the year. Admission charged.

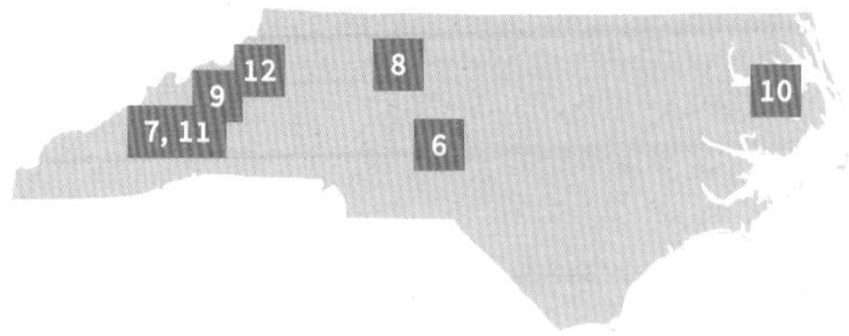

6 Museum of North Carolina Traditional Pottery

127 E. Main St., Seagrove, NC 27341; 336-873-7887
seagrovepotterymuseum.net

Learn about the rich pottery heritage and tradition through items made in and around the Seagrove area for hundreds of years. The museum is a good first stop before visiting the pottery shops in the area—more than 100 from which to choose. Pick up a map of locations, as well as information about special events, such as the annual Seagrove Pottery Festival. Closed January 1, Thanksgiving, and December 24–25. Free admission; donations appreciated.

7 North Carolina Glass Center

140 Roberts St., Ste. C, Asheville, NC 28801; 828-505-3552
ncglasscenter.org

Along with its multi-week courses, North Carolina Glass Center offers the perfect chance for day trippers to create their own work of art with its 30 Minute Make Your Own classes. Participants receive one-on-one guided instruction to create a special glass keepsake in the hot shop, or glassblowing studio. Choose from making a paperweight, ornament, or drinking glass. Or select a 30-minute experience to create beads, pendants, or marbles. The cost of the half-hour class ranges from $50 to $80. Closed January 1, Thanksgiving, and December 25.

8 The Olio

918 Bridge St. NW, Winston-Salem, NC 27101; 336-406-2937
theolio.org

The Olio is a nonprofit glassblowing studio that makes 100% of its glassware from recycled waste glass. It opened in 2014 and offers workshops that last between 2 and 3 hours. Hot shop classes are available September–May by appointment and cost $25–$90. Many classes are open to children as young as 8 (when accompanied by an adult).

9 Penland School of Craft

67 Doras Trail, Penland, NC 28765; 828-765-2359
penland.org

Visitors may explore the grounds of the prestigious Penland School of Craft, known as an international craft center; browse the Penland Gallery and Visitors Center; or stop at The Barns, which contain the studios of Penland's resident artists. While classes are in session, the teaching studios are off-limits. Instruction in clay, drawing, glass, iron, metals, photography, printmaking, letterpress, textiles, and wood is offered in workshops of one-, two-, or eight-week sessions. The gallery is open March–early December, Tuesday–Sunday; closed January 1, Thanksgiving, and December 25. Campus tours are available on Wednesday; reservations required.

10 Pocosin Arts School of Fine Craft

201 Main St., Columbia, NC 27925; 252-796-2787
pocosinarts.org

Pocosin Arts offers a wide range of programs, including weekend workshops and six-week classes that run 2–3 hours each week. Instruction at Pocosin Arts covers textiles, metals and jewelry, painting and drawing, clay, and more. It has offered a teaching studio and gallery on Columbia's Main Street since 1995.

11 River Arts District

Asheville, NC 28801; 828-552-4723
riverartsdistrict.com

Working artist studios are open year-round in Asheville's River Arts District (RAD). It's especially gratifying to find beautiful items and to also have the opportunity to converse with their makers. Check the calendar for special events, classes, and information about the annual Studio Stroll. The RAD is home to more than 200 artists who create using a wide variety of media. Hours vary.

12 Southern Highland Craft Guild Shop at Moses Cone Manor

6570 Blue Ridge Pkwy, Blowing Rock, NC 28605; 828-295-7938
southernhighlandguild.org/shops-and-fairs/moses-cone-manor

The former home of Moses and Bertha Cone, which they called Flat Top Manor, now welcomes visitors who enjoy the stunning views from

the front porch, as well as the exquisite arts and crafts sold inside. Moses was known as The Denim King for the textiles produced at Cone Mills Corporation. The Southern Highland Craft Guild, along with the National Park Service, offers pottery, woven garments, and a variety of other handmade crafts for sale. Located at milepost 294 along the Blue Ridge Parkway. Open April–November, daily.

13 STARworks NC

100 Russell Dr., Star, NC 27356; 910-428-9001
starworksnc.org

STARworks offers 2- to 6-hour classes throughout the year where you can make your own mug or bowl. Class registration must be completed in advance—no walk-ins. STARworks is located near Seagrove, which is recognized as one of the largest pottery communities in the country.

14 Tryon Arts & Crafts School

373 Harmon Field Road, Tryon, NC 28782; 828-859-8323
tryonartsandcrafts.org

Housed in a renovated schoolhouse, Tryon Arts & Crafts School offers professional studios and training in fiber arts, pottery, silver, jewelry, woodworking, lapidary (art of cutting gems), multimedia, and blacksmithing. Most of the classes here are offered in six-week sessions, but it does have one- and two-day workshops, as well as 2- or 3-hour classes. Keep an eye on its website for the current offerings.

Browse the offerings at North Carolina's many arts and crafts schools.
(photographed by Marla Milling)

The free Bigfoot Festival in Marion has food, crafts, and contests.
(photographed by Marla Milling)

PICK JUST ABOUT ANY MONTH in North Carolina, and you're sure to find a festival to attend. There are beer festivals, food festivals, craft festivals, music festivals—even festivals celebrating Bigfoot, Mayberry, and NASCAR. It's impossible to detail every festival in this book, so I've chosen some of the most unusual and/or most popular ones to focus on. You'll find details about some of the state's food-related festivals in Foodie Delights (see page 15).

FOR THE YOUNG AT HEART:

Festivals

Brightly colored hot-air balloons fill the sky in October in Statesville.

1 Asheville Spring Herb Festival

Western North Carolina Farmers Market, 570 Brevard Road, Asheville, NC 28806; 828-301-8968
ashevilleherbfestival.org

Thoughts of this festival are what get me through the cold days of winter. I always arrive bright and early, ready to pick out a bounty of herbs, including my favorite chocolate mint, pineapple sage, and different varieties of basil. The festival tagline is "If it's herbs, it's here," and that's the truth—find exotic plants, herbs, heirloom vegetables, soaps, tinctures, oils, and medicinals. Master gardeners are also on hand to answer questions and provide advice. The festival runs over three days the first weekend in May. Free admission.

2 Carolina BalloonFest

531 Old Airport Road, Statesville, NC 28677; 704-818-3307
carolinaballoonfest.com

This festival offers eye candy with its colorful balloons floating in the air. If you want to stay closer to the ground, try out a tethered balloon ride. The festival takes place over three days in October and features food, live entertainment, and more. The decision on whether to inflate the balloons is weather dependent. Admission and parking charged; separate fee for balloon rides; age 12 and younger free.

3 The Carolina Renaissance Festival & Artisan Marketplace

16445 Poplar Tent Road, Huntersville, NC 28078; 704-896-5555
carolina.renfestinfo.com

More than 500 costumed characters provide fun photo opportunities. Additional attractions include 14 stages of music and other entertainment, knights jousting on horseback, faire games, and more than 100 vendors in the Village Artisan Marketplace. Open October–November, Saturday–Sunday. Admission charged.

4 Coon Dog Day

Downtown Saluda, NC 28773; 828-749-3789
cityofsaludanc.com/coon-dog-day-1

Organizers of many North Carolina festivals ask you to leave your four-legged friends at home. That's not the case for this annual festival in Saluda. Dogs are welcome as long as they are leashed. Coon Dog Day is billed as "a celebration for dogs and their people." Activities include a 5K race, live music, a quirky parade, a street dance, and an American Kennel Club–licensed show. Held in July. Free admission; registration fee for race and show.

5 Folkmoot Festival

Various locations in Western North Carolina; 828-452-2997
folkmoot.org

Folkmoot is a long-running festival headquartered in Waynesville that brings seven to nine international dance teams to Western North Carolina each July. The goal is to celebrate diversity and cultural differences and create a global bond through friendships. The idea of such a folk festival came to Dr. Clinton Border in 1973 as he traveled with a local square dance group to a folk festival in England. He came home with a plan to create an international folk festival here. He traveled to a range of folk festivals, researched how they work, and finally in 1983 proposed his idea to town leaders. Within a month, they embraced his idea, and Folkmoot USA was born. The 10-day festival kicks off with a Parade of Nations on Main Street in Waynesville. During the week, the dance groups perform at multiple venues in the region, and then they return at the end of the festival to Main Street in Waynesville for International Festival Day, a street party with international crafts, music, and food. Separate admission charged for each performance.

6 Grandfather Mountain Highland Games and Gathering O' Scottish Clans

MacRae Meadows at Grandfather Mountain, 2050 Blowing Rock Hwy., Linville, NC 28646; 828-733-1333
gmhg.org

Held in July each year on MacRae Meadows at Grandfather Mountain, this long-running festival started in 1955. Competitions take place in Highland dancing, piping, drumming, Scottish athletic events, track and field events, fiddling, and Scottish harp. Learn more about history and genealogy at clan tents. There's also sheepherding, a children's Highland wrestling competition, Celtic music, and more over the course of four days. Single-day, multiday, and single event tickets with and without shuttle rides are available; visit the website for parking locations.

7 LEAF Festival

377 Lake Eden Road, Black Mountain, NC 28711 (parking at 730 Old US 70, Swannanoa, NC 28778); 828-686-8742
theleaf.org/the-festival

For more than 20 years, the LEAF Festival has served as a biannual event for an intergenerational community. The event (held in May and October) showcases lots of music, camping, arts and crafts, and culture. In recent years, organizers have extended the reach to include a festival in August in downtown Asheville. Single-day and multiday tickets available.

8 Mayberry Days

218 Rockford St., Mount Airy, NC 27030; 336-786-7998
surryarts.org/mayberrydays

For more than 30 years, this fun festival held in late September has brought *The Andy Griffith Show* to life. Enjoy experiencing Mayberry with shows and special performances, a parade, a silent auction, contests, and games. Separate admission charged for each show.

9 NASCAR Day Festival

Main St., Randleman, NC 27317; 336-495-1100
randlemanchamber.com/nascar-day-festival

Randleman is the home of NASCAR legend Richard Petty, known as The King, and three other Hall of Famers: Lee Petty, Dale Inman, and Maurice Petty. The NASCAR Day Festival launched in 1989 as a way to pay tribute to the town's NASCAR and community heritage. Held in October, the festival offers food, music, and, of course, cars. Free admission, but fee applies to some activities.

10 PirateFest

Evans St., Greenville, NC 27858; 252-561-8400 or 252-551-6947
piratefestnc.com

Arrr, matey! Don your pirate costumes and head to the banks of the Tar River for a swashbuckling good time. This two-day festival takes place each April and fills more than eight city blocks on Evans Street.

Activities consist of sword fighting and a pirate encampment, and fine arts and street food vendors offer their wares. There's also a free concert. Free admission.

11 Tom Dooley & Southern Culture Day

11929 NC 268 W, Ferguson, NC 28624; 336-973-3237
whippoorwillacademy.com/tom-dooley-day

Remember that song "Tom Dooley" ("Hang down your head, Tom Dooley")? The town of Ferguson remembers the anniversary of Tom Dula's hanging with Tom Dooley & Southern Culture Day in May. He was put to death for the murder of his girlfriend, Laura Foster, more than 150 years ago, though some historians believe he was wrongly convicted. Learn about the genealogy of Dula (often spelled Dooley), take part in contests for kids and adults, and meet local authors. The event also includes arts and crafts and live music, as well as demonstrations of blacksmithing, woodworking, clogging, and more. Admission charged.

12 White Squirrel Festival

175 E. Main St., Brevard, NC 28712; 828-884-3278
whitesquirrelfestival.com

Brevard is home to a sizable population of white squirrels—they are so popular that a festival was created to celebrate them. Held over two and a half days each May, it's been recognized for selecting undiscovered and regional musical talent. Activities include a Memorial Parade, a White Squirrel Photo Contest, and a White Squirrel 5K and 10K. Free admission.

13 WNC Bigfoot Festival

Main St., Marion, NC 28752
facebook.com/wncbigfootfestival

The WNC Bigfoot Festival in Marion debuted in September 2018. Organizers had hoped that at least 1,000 people would attend. They were blown away when more than 25,000 flocked to town. Even as elusive as Bigfoot is, the creature is ultra popular. Along with festival food, craft vendors, and store windows decorated with fun paintings of Sasquatch, skilled Bigfoot hunters share their castings, photos, and experiences. There's also a Bigfoot Calling Contest and Bigfoot Knocking Competition. This festival is a true gem. Free admission.

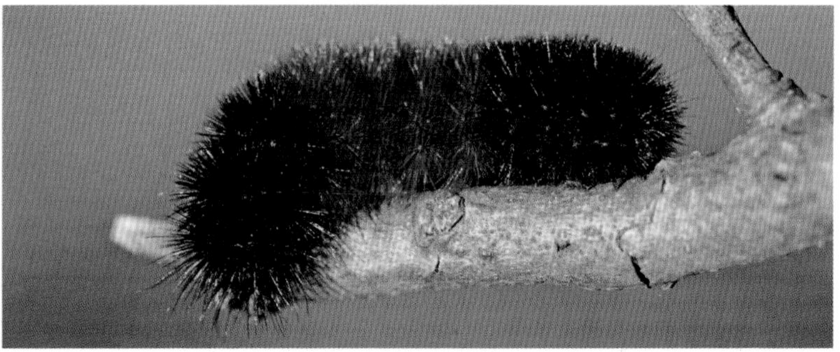

Woolly worms are the stars of the show at Banner Elk's annual festival.

14 Woolly Worm Festival

185 Azalea Cir., Banner Elk, NC 28604; 828-898-5605
woollyworm.com

It's said that woolly worms are great weather forecasters. Woolly worms have 13 body segments, corresponding to the 13 weeks of winter. Each band of color reportedly predicts what that week's weather will be like. As the legend goes, the darker a segment gets, the greater the chance of cold and snow. In late October cheer for the winning worms at the woolly worm races, and enjoy a variety of crafts, food, and entertainment. Admission charged.

Flower Festivals

Fayetteville Dogwood Festival
Festival Park, 335 Ray Ave., Fayetteville, NC 28301; 910-323-1934
thedogwoodfestival.com

Garden Jubilee Festival
Main St., Hendersonville, NC 28792; 828-693-9708
visithendersonvillenc.org/garden-jubilee

NC Rhododendron Festival
Bakersville, NC 28705
ncrhododendronfestival.org

North Carolina Azalea Festival
Wilmington, NC 28401; 910-794-4650
ncazaleafestival.org

Brevard celebrates its population of rare white squirrels each May.

Spend some time playing a board game with friends and family.

NORTH CAROLINA offers amusement parks and outdoor fun, including slipping and sliding at water parks. Board game cafés—along with spots to play old-school pinball and classic arcade games and other places where you can try to solve clues to find your way out of a locked room—are great on days when the weather is less than desirable.

FOR THE YOUNG AT HEART:
Fun & Games

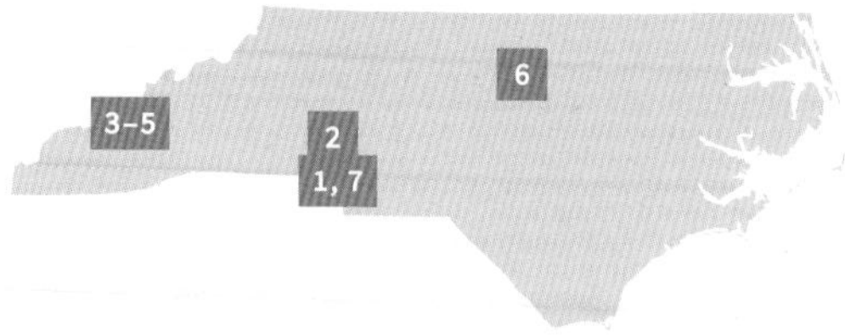

1 Abari Game Bar

1721 N. Davidson St., Charlotte, NC 28206; 980-430-4587
abarigamebar.com

This bar serves up craft beers and specialty cocktails, but it also caters to those who enjoy turning off their phones and going back in time a bit to celebrate vintage arcade games and pinball machines. The game bar also has couches, where you can kick back and play classic console games.

2 All Around the Board Game Cafe

18047 W. Catawba Ave., Ste. E, Cornelius, NC 28031; 980-231-5515
aatbgamecafe.com

Pay a flat fee to gain access to more than 350 games. Play an old classic or try a new one. The café has games for all ages. Special events, including murder mystery dinners, are held throughout the year. It also offers summer camps, birthday parties, a gift shop, and a snack bar.

3 Asheville Pinball Museum

1 Battle Square, Ste. 1B, Asheville, NC 28801; 828-776-5671
ashevillepinball.com

The games are old-school in this fun "museum" of pinball machines and vintage video games, like the all-time most successful game: *Pac-Man*. Founder T. C. DiBella was a middle school teacher when he got the idea of opening a place where people could play pinball and arcade games for one flat fee—no need for rolls of quarters here. Just pay at the door, and all the machines (with the exception of two) are set to free play. You might think that with the advent of video game apps on smartphones and laptops, the idea of playing arcade games would be out of style, but think again. The place stays packed and often has a waiting list for players who are eager to spend some time inside. Closed Tuesdays, January 1, Thanksgiving, and December 25.

4 Asheville Retrocade

800 Haywood Road #100, Asheville, NC 28806; 828-575-9488
ashevilleretrocade.com

Play all day for one low price. Admission provides access to more than 5,000 video games, pinball machines, billiards, Skee-Ball, Foosball, and retro music. Beer, wine, and soft drinks are served. All ages are welcome until 9 p.m. Then 9 p.m.–2 a.m., you have to be 21 or older to enter.

5 Breakout Games–Asheville

60 Patton Ave., Asheville, NC 28801; 828-201-2600
breakoutgames.com/asheville

If you love hunting for clues and don't mind the feeling of being locked in a room with a timer counting down, you'll probably enjoy the latest craze: escape rooms. In Asheville, Breakout Games offers an assortment of room themes that will test your problem-solving and sleuthing skills to see if you can make it out before the time (1 hour) is up. Choose from Mystery Mansion, Museum Heist, The Kidnapping, Operation: Casino, Hostage, or Runaway Train.

6 Bull City Escape

711 Iredell St., Durham, NC 27705; 919-627-8386
bullcityescape.com

There are codes to break, puzzles to solve, and clues to discover. If you succeed within an hour, you'll find the key that will unlock the door and release you from your entrapment. This escape room offers private bookings, which means you will only be paired with family and friends as you try to find the solution. The rooms are rated by difficulty.

7 Carowinds

300 Carowinds Blvd., Charlotte, NC 28273; 704-588-2600
carowinds.com

One of the newest things at this popular amusement park is the Carolinas' first double launch coaster called Copperhead Strike. Carowinds also boasts two of the tallest steel coasters in North America, and with a variety of other coasters, it comes in fifth in the world for the most roller coasters located in a single park. Guests also find a range of thrill rides, family rides, and rides designed for younger kids, as well as a water park. Buy tickets for the day, or if you're close enough to visit often, a season pass provides free parking and unlimited visits. Open April and August–October, Friday–Sunday; May, Thursday–Sunday; Memorial Day–mid-August, daily; closed November–March.

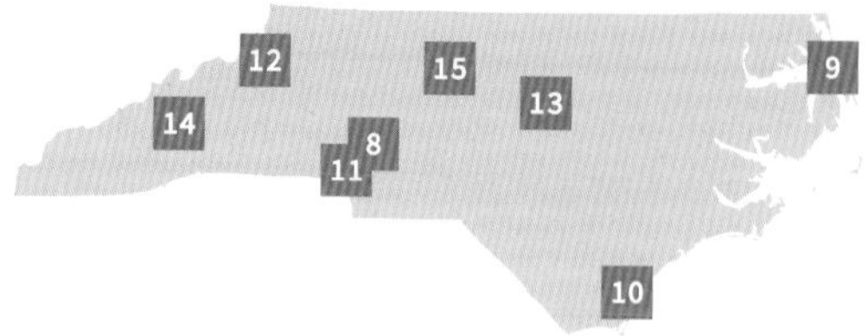

8 Great Wolf Lodge

10175 Weddington Road, Concord, NC 28027; 866-925-9653
greatwolf.com/concord

You don't need to check the weather report before heading to this fun water park. Most of the slipping and sliding takes place indoors. Some of the features include a water fort tree house, a tandem tube ride that travels four stories, toboggan-style water racing, and an outdoor activity pool known as the Raccoon Lagoon. Access to the water park is exclusive to overnight guests.

9 H20BX Waterpark

8526 Caratoke Hwy., Powells Point, NC 27966; 252-491-3000
h2obxwaterpark.com

This Outer Banks water park offers about 20 rides, plus more relaxing attractions such as a wave pool and beach. Purchase a ticket for a single day, or grab season passes, a great value if you're close enough to make good use of them.

10 Jungle Rapids Family Fun Park

5320 Oleander Dr., Wilmington, NC 28403; 910-791-0666
junglerapids.com

Float in the lazy river, race go-carts, play arcade games, enjoy a round of laser tag or minigolf, and take part in other fun activities at this bustling park. There's a full-service restaurant as well. The water park is open mid-June–late August. The dry park is open year-round (hours vary). The water park charges separate admission; individual tickets (or combo packages) are required for the dry park activities.

11 Lucky's Bar & Arcade

300 N. College St. #104, Charlotte, NC 28202; 704-342-2557
luckycharlotte.com

Head back to the '90s when you enter this bar and arcade. Classic arcade games include *Galaga, Frogger, Dig Dug, Space Invaders,* and, of course, *Pac-Man's Arcade Party* and *Ms. Pac-Man.* You'll also find multiple versions of Nintendo, Sega Genesis, and Xbox, along with air hockey, Foosball, pinball, and more. Special events are held throughout the year.

12 Tweetsie Railroad

300 Tweetsie Railroad Lane, Blowing Rock, NC 28605; 828-264-9061
tweetsie.com

The star of the show at this delightful Wild West theme park (North Carolina's oldest) is *Tweetsie,* a No. 12 steam engine. Tweetsie Railroad opened in the summer of 1957. Guests can take a 3-mile loop train ride, watch live shows, visit the Deer Park Zoo, and soak in the Wild West flavor. Special events include the Ghost Train and Tweetsie Christmas. Open April–May and late August–October, Friday–Sunday; Memorial Day–late August, daily; late November–December, Friday–Saturday nights.

13 VR Junkies

1105 Walnut St., Cary, NC 27511; 919-249-5987
vrjunkies.com/raleigh

Discover the cutting-edge technology of virtual reality. Choose from a wide mix of games, including sports games, *Cowbots and Aliens* (not a typo), *Google Earth VR, Fruit Ninja VR, Lightblade VR, Project Cars 2,* and others. Pricing is based on 10-minute increments up to 2 hours.

14 Well Played Board Game Café

58 Wall St., Asheville, NC 28801; 828-232-7375
wellplayedasheville.com

Well Played Board Game Café has the largest board game library in North Carolina—more than 600 games in all. Choose among new games like Catan, Pandemic, and Ticket to Ride, or select a classic such as Monopoly, Sorry!, Scrabble, Clue, or Risk. Pay a small fee to play as long as you want. Game masters can help you with the rules or strategies. The café also has a fun menu of sandwiches, snacks, desserts, and beverages.

15 Wet 'n Wild Emerald Pointe

3910 S. Holden Road, Greensboro, NC 27406; 336-852-9721
emeraldpointe.com

Situated on 41 acres, this popular water park offers more than 20 water rides and more than 3 million gallons of water. If you want to take things slow, just float down the lazy river. For the more adventurous, check out the Daredevil Drop—you drop 76 feet on a steep water chute. The park has a great selection of fun water activities. Rent a cabana to enjoy a shaded retreat throughout the day.

At Hands On! Children's Museum, kids can climb a mountain and view a waterfall. (photographed by Sam Dean/Distl PR)

FORGET MUSEUMS WITH SIGNS that say DO NOT TOUCH. In these family-friendly museums, hands-on experimentation is applauded and encouraged. Kids' museums across the state offer immersive experiences, interactive exhibits, and learning opportunities to enhance a child's growth and development.

FOR THE YOUNG AT HEART:
Kids' Museums

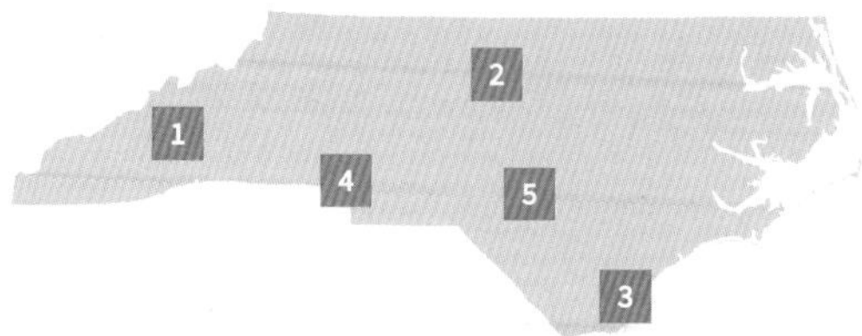

1 Asheville Museum of Science

43 Patton Ave., Asheville, NC 28801; 828-254-7162
ashevillescience.org

Once known as the Burnham S. Colburn Memorial Museum, the museum changed its name and scope twice before becoming the Asheville Museum of Science (AMOS) when it opened in a new location at 43 Patton Ave. in downtown Asheville on November 11, 2016. But the legacy of engineer and bank president Burnham Standish Colburn hasn't been forgotten. The facility includes the Colburn Hall of Minerals, as well as a STEM (science, technology, engineering, and math) lab, the AMOS Mars Rover, the Terrabox elevation simulator (which brings topography maps to life), a hurricane simulator, and many other exhibits. Closed January 1, Memorial Day, July 4, Labor Day, Thanksgiving, and December 25. Admission charged.

2 Children's Museum of Alamance County

217 S. Main St., Graham, NC 27253; 336-228-7997
childrensmuseumofalamance.org

Hands-on exhibits include the Building Zone, Artist's Workshop, Health Center, Science Adventure, Wobble & Roll (for infants and

Kids can "fish" in the Haw River or climb the Unity Dome at the Children's Museum of Alamance County. (courtesy of the Children's Museum of Alamance County)

toddlers), and My Own Backyard (which features a river for "fishing" and fossil excavation). Check the online calendar for special events. Closed Sunday and Monday. Admission charged.

3 The Children's Museum of Wilmington

116 Orange St., Wilmington, NC 28401; 910-254-3534
playwilmington.org

I have so many wonderful memories of taking my children to this museum when they were younger. They especially loved creating in the Art Studio, playing on the pirate ship, and ringing up customers in the Neighborhood Market. Other hands-on exhibits include such things as the Imagination Playground, Teddy Bear Hospital, and Toddler Treehouse. Housed in three historical buildings, the museum has a really fun, colorful layout covering four floors. Open daily, Memorial Day–Labor Day; closed on Mondays the rest of the year. Admission charged.

4 Discovery Place Science

301 N. Tryon St., Charlotte, NC 28202; 704-372-6261
science.discoveryplace.org

This is the place to discover some cool stuff, study science, experiment, build, work with others, and learn by practicing. Visitors can explore an indoor rain forest, a bug lab, a *Being Me* exhibit that teaches kids about health and anatomy, and special places for younger kids. Plus, it has an IMAX theater and live shows, such as story time, science demonstrations, and animal shows. Field trips, birthday parties, group visits, Scout programs, and homeschool classes are offered. Closed Easter, Thanksgiving, and December 24–25. Admission charged.

5 Fascinate-U Children's Museum

116 Green St., Fayetteville, NC 28302; 910-829-9171
fascinate-u.com

Fun exhibit areas consist of a market stand, garden plot, grocery store, post office, 911 emergency center, and bakery where kids can do some role-playing and learn new skills. In the construction area kids can use tools and wooden blocks to build things, and one area allows them to experience what it's like to be a judge or lawyer. Closed Monday, January 1, Easter, July 4, Thanksgiving, and December 24–25. Admission charged.

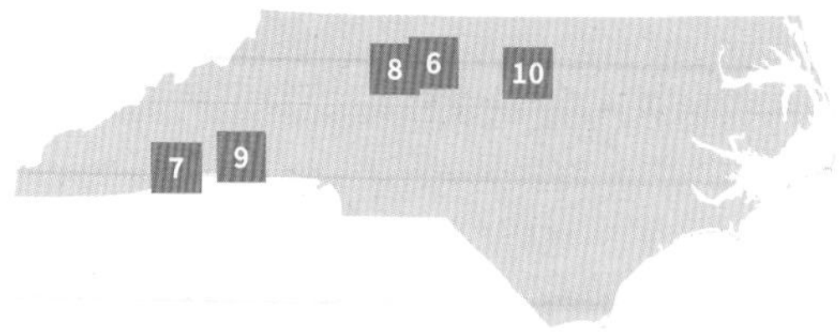

6 Greensboro Children's Museum

220 N. Church St., Greensboro, NC 27401; 336-574-2898
gcmuseum.com

This safe, fun environment provides kids with many hands-on learning opportunities. Jerry Hyman took his dream of having a children's museum in Greensboro to community leaders. It became a reality when it opened on May 15, 1999. In 2009 The Edible Schoolyard opened at the museum. This 0.5-acre organic garden offers teaching opportunities and a kitchen classroom. The latest project, Reaching Greater Heights, involves three phases. The first opened in summer 2017 with an Outdoor Play Plaza addition. The second opened in the fall of 2018 and includes an indoor, interactive water exhibit. The third phase began in 2019 to bring in a technology media exhibit. Open to members only Monday morning. Admission charged.

7 Hands On! Children's Museum

318 N. Main St., Hendersonville, NC 28792; 828-697-8333
handsonwnc.org

You can keep little hands busy in this place. Children can play in more than 12 interactive exhibit areas, such as the Art & Sensory Studio, Grocery Store, Imagination Playground, Pet Vet Hospital, Puppet Theatre, and Rigamajig, which provides access to wooden planks, wheels, nuts and bolts, and pulleys and ropes to build some amazing things. Closed Sunday and Monday, January 1, July 4, Thanksgiving, and December 24–25. Admission charged.

8 Kaleideum

North: 400 W. Hanes Mill Road, Winston-Salem, NC 27105; 336-767-6730
north.kaleideum.org
Downtown: 390 S. Liberty St., Winston-Salem, NC 27101; 336-723-9111
downtown.kaleideum.org

Kaleideum is the result of a 2016 merger of the Children's Museum of Winston-Salem and SciWorks. There are two locations: one in downtown Winston-Salem, featuring fused STEM (science, technology, engineering, and math) exhibits and programming, and the other north of the city, which offers hands-on learning with its seven indoor science halls, planetarium, and Environmental Park habitats. Check the individual websites for special events. Closed January 1, Easter, Thanksgiving, and December 25. The North location is also closed on Monday, Labor Day–May only; the Downtown location is only open to members on Monday morning, Labor Day–May, and is closed the first Monday of the month, October–May. Admission charged.

9 KidSenses and The Factory

172 N. Main St., Rutherfordton, NC 28139; 828-286-2120
The Factory (opens 2020): 151 Taylor St., Rutherfordton, NC 28139
kidsenses.org and factorymuseum.org

A big expansion is underway at the KidSenses learning museum in downtown Rutherfordton. Within the year 2020, the facility will expand by 9,500 square feet with the addition of The Factory, which will be located in a building behind the KidSenses museum. The campus also includes a 7,500-square-foot outdoor discovery garden. KidSenses, which opened in 2004, is a 10,000-square-foot space geared to families with children up to the age of 10. The Factory is themed after the growing Maker Movement and will attract older kids, teens, and adults as they gather to make things. The Factory will consist of five main areas: the Factory Gallery, Tech Lab (equipped with computers, 3-D printers, and laser cutters), the Make It Place (stocked with power and manual tools), the Food Studio with a fully functioning kitchen, and an Idea Zone for collaboration and team building. Closed Sunday–Monday. Admission charged.

10 Kidzu Children's Museum

201 S. Estes Dr., Chapel Hill, NC 27514; 919-933-1455
kidzuchildrensmuseum.org

STEM (science, technology, engineering, and math) education is the focus here. That mission is supported with interactive play, inventive exhibits, and a variety of sensory experiences. Spend time getting hands dirty in the Outdoor Learning Garden, stretch the imagination in the Flexible Forest and Forest Theater, and promote a love of reading in the Book Nook. The Makery allows guests of all ages to create crafts. Each month Makery Masters are on hand to share their expertise. They range from artists and craftspeople to inventors and scientists. Closed Monday, January 1, Easter, Thanksgiving, and December 24–25. Admission charged.

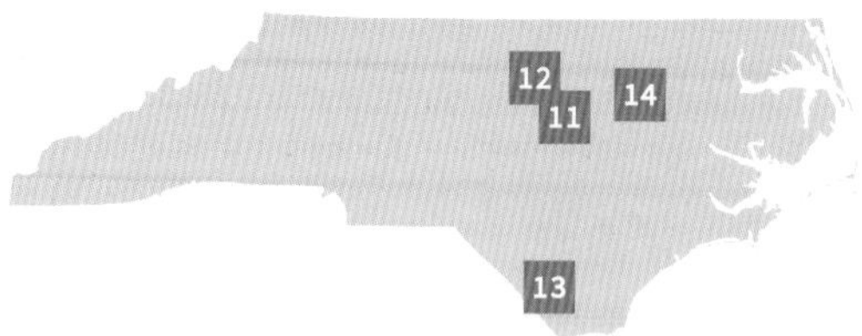

11 Marbles Kids Museum

201 E. Hargett St., Raleigh, NC 27601; 919-834-4040
marbleskidsmuseum.org

This museum provides an interactive space for parents and kids to play together. It first opened on September 29, 2007, and continues to wow visitors with a range of hands-on activities located inside and outside. Kids can create, dance, build, discover, climb, tumble, and twirl. Best of all, they'll be learning, or "using their marbles," to figure things out. Closed Easter, Thanksgiving, and December 24–25. Admission charged; discounted rates on Thursday afternoons and first Friday afternoons.

12 Museum of Life + Science

433 W. Murray Ave., Durham, NC 27704; 919-220-5429
lifeandscience.org

One thing is for sure—there are so many activities here that there's no chance of your kids getting bored. The site is comprised of 84 acres containing more than 60 species of animals, an interactive science center, and one of the largest butterfly houses on the East Coast. Keep an eye on the calendar for special events, camps, classes, and pop-up exhibits. Closed Monday, Labor Day–Memorial Day. Admission charged.

13 North Carolina Museum of Natural Sciences–Whiteville

415 S. Madison St., Whiteville, NC 28472; 910-914-4185
naturalsciences.org/visit/whiteville

Intergenerational learning takes shape here with opportunities to learn about the natural world and the wonders it contains. Exhibits include an Investigative Lab, Naturalist Center, Nature PlaySpace, Discovery Forest, In Your Backyard Resource Center, and a Distance Learning Classroom. Closed Sunday and Monday. Free admission; donations appreciated.

14 Rocky Mount Imperial Centre

270 Gay St., Rocky Mount, NC 27804; 252-972-1266
imperialcentre.org

Repurposed buildings that once housed the Imperial Tobacco Company and the old Braswell Memorial Library now offer space for an arts center, children's museum and science center, and a performing arts theater covering 135,000 square feet in all. There are a variety of permanent exhibits and special temporary exhibits, plus classes and workshops covering drawing, painting, ceramics, and more for artists of all ages and levels. Closed Monday, January 1, Good Friday, Easter, and December 24–25. Admission charged.

In June or September, take a tour down the yellow brick road at the Land of Oz. (photographed by Marla Milling)

FOR THOSE SEEKING IDEAS for discovering the more unusual side of what North Carolina has to offer, there are many curiosities, humorous attractions, and baffling experiences that will leave you scratching your head as you try to figure them out. Some are easy to find. Others may require you to stop and ask for directions along the way (don't always trust GPS).

FOR THE YOUNG AT HEART:
Weird & Wacky

Walk along the Urban Trail in Asheville, which reveals the city's history along the way.

1 *Aluminum Tree & Aesthetically Challenged Seasonal Ornament Museum and Research Center* at the Transylvania Heritage Museum

189 W. Main St., Brevard, NC 28712; 828-884-2347
transylvaniaheritage.org/content/aluminum-christmas-tree-museum

Every year from early November to late December, the Transylvania Heritage Museum in downtown Brevard delights visitors with a unique display of aluminum trees and ornaments. It's a throwback to the 1950s when this type of tree was popular. The exhibit showcases more than two dozen trees. It all started in 1991 when a local home designer received an aluminum tree as a gag gift. Steven Jackson embraced the gift by throwing a party and inviting guests to bring equally quirky ornaments. Friends continued giving him trees until he had too many to fit in his house. They are now on display seasonally at the museum for others to enjoy. Open early November–late December, Wednesday–Saturday.

2 American Museum of the House Cat

4704 US 441 S, Sylva, NC 28779; 828-476-9376
catman2.org/the-american-museum-of-the-house-cat.html

An incredible private collection of all things cat-related is on display in Sylva at the American Museum of the House Cat. It features items collected by Dr. Harold Sims (his alias is CatMan2) over a period of more than 30 years. The building is stuffed with vintage ads featuring cats, fine art, cat posters, cat figurines, folk art, toys, and more items than can even be imagined. Closed Monday. Admission charged; fees help support a nearby no-kill cat shelter.

3 Brown Mountain Lights

ncpedia.org/brown-mountain-lights

For more than a century, many people have reported witnessing strange, unexplained lights on Brown Mountain. The lights appear spontaneously and are said to even change colors at times. Various theories exist about the cause of these lights, but no one has ever found a definitive reason. There are different spots where people claim to see the mysterious lights, but one of the most popular is along NC 181 at mile marker 20. Brown Mountain is in the Pisgah National Forest on the border of Burke and Caldwell Counties.

4 Fields of the Wood

10000 NC 294, Murphy, NC 28906; 828-494-7855
cogop.org/fow

The Ten Commandments take center stage on Burger Mountain in Murphy. Each commandment appears in letters so big that planes can read the words from 5,000 feet. Each letter is 5 feet high and 4 feet wide. A staircase leads between the commandments—five are listed on each side. If you have the stamina to reach the top (326 stairs), long-distance mountain views await. A café and gift shop are also on-site. Open daily, sunrise–sunset. Free admission; donations appreciated.

5 Johns River House of Mugs

2085–2199 Old Johns River Road, Collettsville, NC 28611

You might have to stop and ask some locals how to get to the Cup House, which is a private residence. It's at the end of a country road in Collettsville, and GPS doesn't turn up reliable directions. Avery and Doris Sisk started decorating their house with mugs they picked up at a flea market about 20 years ago. They kept adding mugs through the years and have now covered the exterior in more than 25,000 cups. Some have been added by visitors. There's no charge, but donations are appreciated.

6 Judaculla Rock

552 Judaculla Rock Road, Cullowhee, NC 28723; 828-293-3053
rec.jacksonnc.org/judaculla-rock

Petroglyphs (carvings and drawings) cover this mysterious soapstone boulder in Jackson County. Cherokee legend says a giant named Judaculla left the markings. Like the Brown Mountain Lights, many different theories have emerged over the years, but no one has ever fully unraveled the mystery. One vandal was arrested after defacing the rock in 2016; erosion has also caused damage, making it difficult to study.

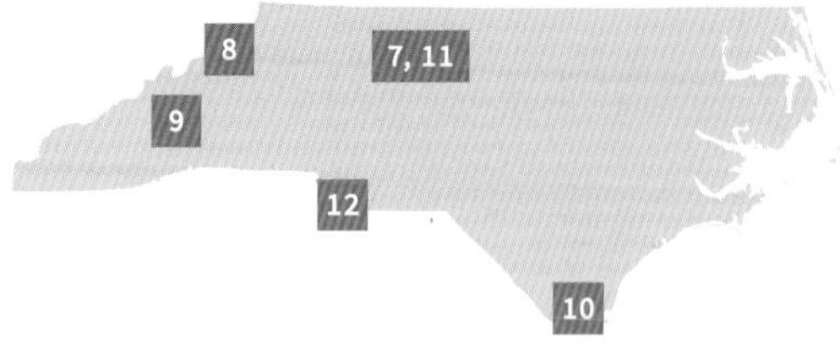

7 Körner's Folly

413 S. Main St., Kernersville, NC 27284; 336-996-7922
kornersfolly.org

Construction on this unusual place began in 1878. Jule Gilmer Körner—an interior decorator, furniture designer, and painter—envisioned it as a place to illustrate his work to potential clients. The home was continually renovated to show off his latest designs. And as you can imagine, a decorator's showroom has an array of features: all of the doorways, windows, and 15 fireplaces are distinctively different. The house has 22 rooms, three floors, and seven levels. The top level has a private theater. The house was named Körner's Folly after Körner learned that his neighbor thought the design was frivolous and odd. Closed Monday and Tuesday, January 1, Easter, July 4, Thanksgiving, December 24, December 25, and December 31. Admission charged.

8 Land of Oz

889 Elderberry Ridge Road, Beech Mountain, NC 28604; 800-514-3849
landofoznc.com

A once popular theme park sits empty much of the year, but it comes back to life for special occasions. The park welcomes paying visitors to its annual Autumn at Oz Festival (in September) and Journey with Dorothy tours (in June). The Land of Oz first opened on June 15, 1970. Actress Debbie Reynolds cut the opening-day ribbon with her teenage daughter, Carrie Fisher (Princess Leia in *Star Wars*), by her side. The park became an overnight sensation, with more than 400,000 people traveling the yellow brick road that first season. A series of obstacles led to the decision to close the park at the end of the 1980 season. In the mid-1990s, the Autumn at Oz Festival was created to allow people a glimpse of this magical mountaintop park. The park is only open for special ticketed events.

9 LaZoom Bus Tours

76 Biltmore Ave., Asheville, NC 28801; 828-225-6932
lazoomtours.com

Get on a quirky purple bus in Asheville and experience a hilarious, wacky trip through Asheville's history, as guides keep you laughing with zany comedy and fun facts. You might even spot the owner, Jim Lauzon, as Sister Bad Habit, a nun who rides a super-tall red bike beside the bus on certain tours. Choose from a City Comedy Tour, Haunted Comedy Tour, Band & Beer Tour, and a Kids' Comedy Tour.

10 Mary's Gone Wild Folk Art and Doll Baby Museum

2431 Holden Beach Road SW, Supply, NC 28462; 910-842-9908
marysgonewild.com

Mary Paulsen learned from an early age how to repair dolls. She fixed dolls for neighbors and would even rescue trashed dolls to restore them. She says God gave her the idea in 1996 to create a village in her front yard for her 6,000 dolls. From there, she filled her yard with her own art that she calls "Gonna make you smile art." Her garden has survived many hurricanes. Open daily, year-round. Free admission.

11 The Mickey Coffee Pot

Old Salem Road and S. Main St., Winston-Salem, NC 27101
wachoviahistoricalsociety.org/literature/salemcoffeepot.html

A gigantic coffeepot sits on display in Winston-Salem; its history dates back to 1858. That's when Julius Mickey first displayed the coffeepot on a pole to draw attention to the tinsmith business he operated with his brother, Samuel, at the corner of Belews and South Main Streets. It measures more than 7 feet high and more than 2 feet in diameter at the top, and 5 feet, 4 inches diameter at the base. Legend has it that a Union soldier hid in it during the Civil War. Halloween vandals managed to knock it down several times before it was removed to allow I-40 to come through. It was stored for several years until 1962, when town officials reached an agreement with the owners to display it in its current location.

12 Museum of the Alphabet

6409 Davis Road, Waxhaw, NC 28173; 704-843-6066
jaars.org/experience/museums

You can do a lot with your name at this museum—type it in Braille, translate it in a number of languages, and even see how it would look in Klingon. Educational, interactive exhibits are spread out among 12 galleries; learn about other writing systems and Bible translation. Once

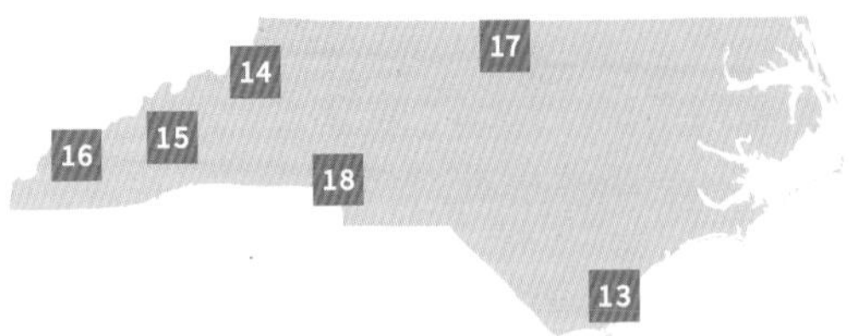

a month, it has a special nighttime program called Night at the Alphabet Museum. This free event is recommended for age 8 and up. Check the website for specific dates. Closed Sunday, January 1, Martin Luther King Jr. Day, Good Friday and Easter weekend, Memorial Day, July 4, Labor Day, Thanksgiving, and December 25. Free admission; donations appreciated.

13 Museum of the Bizarre

201 S. Water St., Wilmington, NC 28401; 910-399-2641
museumbizarre.com

Justin LaNasa has a knack for finding and collecting some of the most bizarre objects you've ever seen. But that didn't go over so well when he got married. His collection was too big to deal with at home, so his wife told him he had two options: trash the collection or open a museum. So he opened Museum of the Bizarre in downtown Wilmington. Visitors can see shrunken heads, a chupacabra hand, Harry Houdini's Ouija board, props from horror movies, and much more. Open daily. Admission charged.

14 Musical Parking Garage

231 E. Seventh St., Charlotte, NC 28202
janneysound.com/project/touch-my-building-charlotte-nc

Imagine a building that can interact with you. That's exactly what happens when pedestrians touch the "light fins" placed around the 7th Street Station Parking Garage in Charlotte. *Touch My Building* is the creation of architect and American sound artist Christopher Janney. When touched, a fin lights up and plays a mix of tones. The music and lights are also programmed to play on the hour, and occasionally they will start playing without being touched—could there be a ghost in the building?

15 Mystery Hill

129 Mystery Hill Lane, Blowing Rock, NC 28605; 828-264-2792
mysteryhill.com

I've taken my kids to this personal favorite many times over the years. The attraction bills itself as a natural gravitational anomaly, where balls roll uphill and water flows uphill. Closed Thanksgiving and December 25. Admission here also includes the 1903 Dougherty House Museum, The Moon Mullin's Native American Artifacts Museum, The Appalachian Fossil and Dinosaur Museum, Bubblerama, and more.

16 Pritchard Park Drum Circle

67 Patton Ave, Asheville, NC 28801; 828-259-5800
ashevillenc.gov/departments/parks/inventory/default.htm#regional

Drummers begin filling Asheville's Pritchard Park every Friday in warm weather to pound out an organic beat. The drum circle attracts dancers, Hula-Hoopers, curious tourists, and folks who love the colorful array of music and movement. Anyone is welcome to take part; all they need to do is show up with a drum and keep the beat going. Generally occurs every Friday, April–October. Free event.

17 The Road to Nowhere

Lakeview Dr. E, Bryson City, NC 28713; 865-436-1200
greatsmokies.com/road-nowhere or nps.gov/grsm

They say the road to hell is paved with good intentions. Now, this road doesn't lead to hell, but it was created with good intentions. In the 1930s and '40s, during the creation of Fontana Dam and Great Smoky Mountains National Park, Swain County turned over a large chunk of its private land to the federal government. The formation of Fontana Lake flooded Old NC 288, so the government promised to build a new road from Bryson City to Fontana. Construction began on the road but stopped due to environmental concerns. It goes 6 miles into the Great Smoky Mountains National Park before stalling out at a tunnel. While the lack of road prevents further car travel, there are plenty of trails in the area to explore on foot.

18 Shangri-La Stone Village

Henry Warren Road, Prospect Hill, NC 27314

A retired tobacco farmer by the name of Henry L. Warren created a miniature stone town in his side yard. He dubbed it Shangri-La and continued to add buildings until he died in 1977 at the age of 84. In all, he built 27 structures, including a gym, bank, library, hotel, theater, and gas station. The mini village remains located at a private residence, but visitors are welcome.

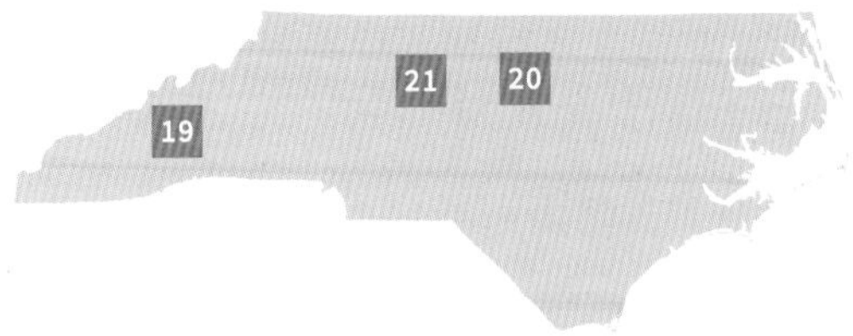

19 Urban Trail

Between Eagle St. and Woodfin St. and Page Ave. and N. Spruce St., Asheville, NC 28801
ashevillenc.gov/departments/community/public_art/urban_trail.htm

Walking around Asheville, you're sure to quickly stumble on some sculptures: a giant iron outside the Flatiron Building, pigs and turkeys at Pack Square Park, cats along Wall Street, and a pair of shoes outside the Thomas Wolfe House Memorial. They are all part of the unique Urban Trail, which highlights the architecture, people, and historic events of Asheville. The trail has 30 stations divided into five categories: The Gilded Age (1880–1930), The Frontier Period (1784–1880), The Times of Thomas Wolfe (1900–1938), The Era of Civic Pride, and The Age of Diversity. A map is available for download.

20 Vincent & Ethel Simonetti Historic Tuba Collection

1825 Chapel Hill Road, Durham, NC 27707; 919-599-3791
simonettitubacollection.com

A visit to this unusual museum requires some advance planning. Appointments must be made at least 24 hours ahead of your visit. Vincent played tuba in the orchestra for the North American tour of the Moiseyev Ballet Company, a Russian folk ballet troupe. He and Ethel began collecting tubas and have amassed more than 300 instruments. Viewing of the tuba collection is by appointment only every Tuesday and Thursday, 3–6 p.m. Free admission; donations appreciated.

21 World's Original Largest Chest of Drawers

508 N. Hamilton St., High Point, NC 27265

High Point is known as the Home Furnishings Capital of the World due to the biannual High Point Market. It's fitting, then, that a gigantic, 38-foot dresser stands in the middle of town. The middle drawer is pulled out a bit, with two neon-colored socks, 6 feet in length, hanging over the edge. In 1999 a nearby furniture store built a chest more than twice as tall, usurping this chest's claim on "world's largest."

Körner's Folly has undergone many drastic renovations since 1878, when it was first built.

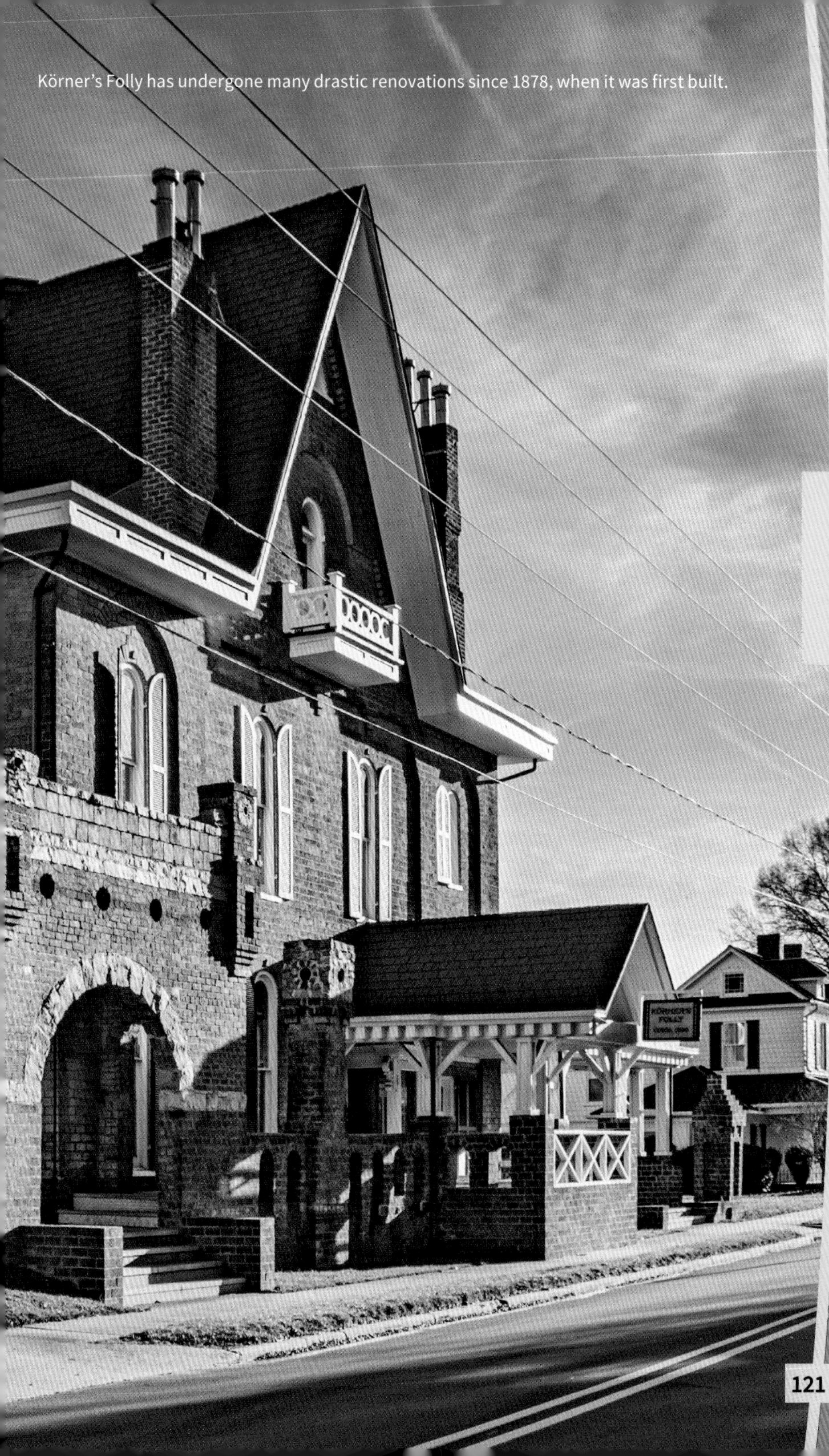

Rare American motorcycles fill the Wheels Through Time Museum.
(courtesy of Wheels Through Time Museum)

YOU CAN CELEBRATE your love for wheeled vehicles—whether it's NASCAR, motorcycles, or big 18-wheelers—as you explore unique museums across North Carolina. There are places to see antique cars, rare American motorcycles, and other types of vehicles. You can also experience the thrill of sitting behind the wheel when you visit the NASCAR Hall of Fame in Charlotte and participate in its racing simulators, or when you take a ride on the Tail of the Dragon.

ON THE GO:
Cars, Motorcycles, & Trucks

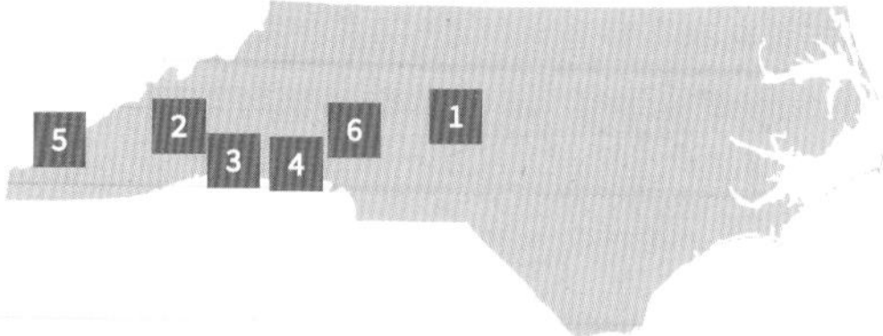

1 American Classic Motorcycle Museum

1170 US 64 W, Asheboro, NC 27205; 336-629-9564
facebook.com/pg/acmmofasheboro

Harley-Davidson fans will love this place. It has one of the largest collections of Harley motorcycles in the country. After examining the bikes on display, take time to visit the gift shop and grab a bite to eat at Heritage Diner. Closed Sunday. Free admission.

2 Antique Car Museum

111 Grovewood Road, Asheville, NC 28804; 828-253-7651
grovewood.com/antique-car-museum

Harry Blomberg, owner of Harry's on the Hill car dealership, founded this museum in 1966. Highlights of the collection include a rare 1957 Cadillac Eldorado Brougham and a 1922 American LaFrance fire truck. Closed January–March, Thanksgiving, and December 25. Free admission; donations appreciated.

3 Bennett Classics Antique Auto Museum

241 Vance St., Forest City, NC 28043; 828-247-1767
bennettclassics.com

Winner of the 2012 Antique Automobile Club of America (AACA) National Museum Award, this museum came into existence in 2007. It contains a wide range of vehicles, everything from classic cars to Mack Trucks to a 1963 Mayberry sheriff's car signed by Don Knotts, who played Deputy Barney Fife on *The Andy Griffith Show*. Closed Saturday–Monday. Admission charged.

4 C. Grier Beam Truck Museum

111 N. Mountain St., Cherryville, NC 28021; 704-435-3072
beamtruckmuseum.com

The Carolina Freight Carriers Corporation founded this museum in 1982 as part of its 50th-anniversary observance. It's housed in the original gas station where Carolina Freight began. There's more than

Carolina Freight, founded in 1932, is celebrated at the C. Grier Beam Truck Museum. (courtesy of the C. Grier Beam Truck Museum)

7,500 square feet of trucking memorabilia to explore. Closed Sunday–Wednesday (except by appointment), January 1, July 4, Thanksgiving, and December 24–25. Free admission.

5 Deals Gap

US 129/Tapoco Road and NC 28, Robbinsville, NC 28771
tailofthedragon.com/events

If you're looking for a rush of adrenaline on your motorcycle or in your sports car, head to the Tail of the Dragon (US 129), also known as Deals Gap, highlighting 318 curves in 11 miles. The season typically runs from early March to mid-November. Check the website above to find out when a particular motorcycle or car club will be in town. The public stretch of road starts in North Carolina and travels into Tennessee.

6 Memory Lane Motorsports & Historical Automotive Museum

769 NC 150/River Hwy., Mooresville, NC 28117; 704-662-3673
memorylaneautomuseum.com

If you love cars, you're sure to find a model here that will thrill you. The museum has more than 150 cars—classic cars including Model Ts and Model As, race cars, drag cars, muscle cars, cars once driven by NASCAR stars, and more. There's also a collection of pedal cars,

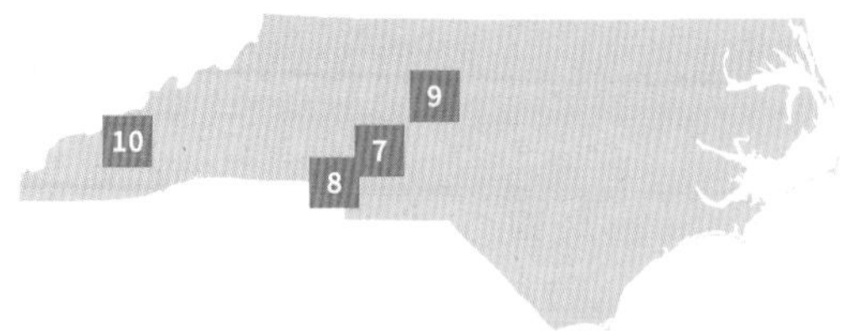

antique toys, motorcycles, and other memorabilia. Learn about the history of the automobile from 1901 to the present, as well as the history of racing. The self-guided tour allows you to go at your own pace. Closed Sunday, January 1, Memorial Day, July 4, Labor Day, Thanksgiving, day after Thanksgiving, and December 24–25. Admission charged.

7 Morrison Motor Car Museum

4545 US 29/Concord Pkwy. S, Concord, NC 28027; 704-788-9500
morrisonmotorco.com/museum/index.php?theme=museum

Located next to the Charlotte Motor Speedway, this museum features more than 50 cars, including classic models and muscle cars. Its 18,000 square feet of space contains a gift shop and banquet facilities. Closed Wednesday and Sunday. Admission charged.

8 NASCAR Hall of Fame

400 E. Martin Luther King Jr. Blvd., Charlotte, NC 28202; 888-902-6463
nascarhall.com

Opened on May 11, 2010, this interactive attraction features hands-on exhibits, artifacts, a theater, the Hall of Honor, a restaurant, and a gift shop. You can get a feel for what it's like behind the wheel with racing simulators, and check out a full-size car transporter for a close-up look at a track car's hub of activity. Galleries tell the story of NASCAR's history. Closed Tuesday (except with group reservations). Admission charged.

9 Petty Museum

309 Branson Mill Road, Randleman, NC 27317; 336-495-1143
rpmuseum.com

Established in 1988, this museum celebrates one of the founding families of stock car racing. Richard Petty became known as The King. His dad, Lee Petty, won three NASCAR Grand Nationals. The family legacy of race car drivers includes Richard's son, Kyle Petty, and his grandson, Adam Petty. Closed Sunday, Thanksgiving, the day after Thanksgiving, and December 24–January 1. Admission charged.

10 Wheels Through Time Museum

62 Vintage Lane, Maggie Valley, NC 28751; 828-926-6266
wheelsthroughtime.com

Housing a premier collection of rare American motorcycles, this museum, which first opened on July 4, 2002, has more than 350 machines from 25 makers, including Harley-Davidson, Excelsior, Flying Merkel, Indian, Pope, Yale, and more. It also contains some unique automobiles. Closed December–March. Closed Tuesday and Wednesday, Easter, and Thanksgiving. Admission charged.

Grovewood Village showcases some beautiful vintage vehicles at the free Antique Car Museum. (photographed by Tim Barnwell; courtesy of the Antique Car Museum/Grovewood Village)

This 60-foot granite monument was dedicated to Wilbur and Orville Wright in 1932. (courtesy of National Park Service/public domain)

AVIATION IS A BIG DEAL in North Carolina, of course, thanks to Orville and Wilbur Wright. They conducted their first successful airplane flights in Kitty Hawk. But North Carolina also has a rich history related to trains and ships. Museums in the state cover everything from the wrecked flagship of Blackbeard the Pirate to rare locomotives and other fascinating artifacts.

ON THE GO:

Trains, Planes, & Ships

The Great Smoky Mountains Railroad travels through scenic parts of the state.

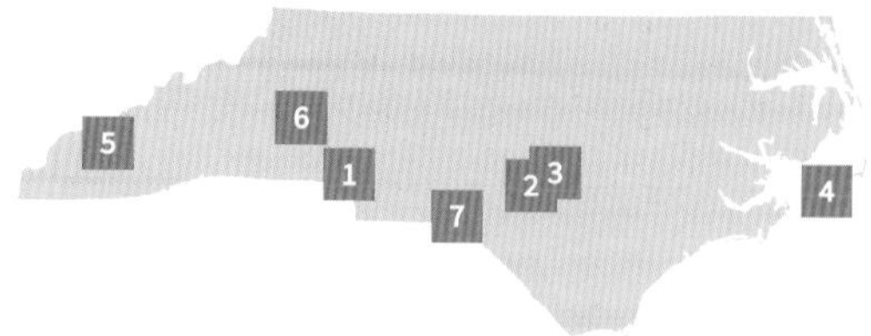

1 Carolinas Aviation Museum

4672 First Flight Dr., Charlotte, NC 28208; 704-997-3770
carolinasaviation.org

Showcasing a wide variety of military, commercial, and civilian aircraft, as well as uniforms, aviation artifacts, books, photographs, and other aviation-related materials, this museum is affiliated with the Smithsonian Institutions. Donations to the collection are appreciated but must go through a formal review process first. Closed January 1, Easter, Thanksgiving, and December 24–25. Admission charged.

2 82d Airborne Division War Memorial Museum

5108 Ardennes St., Bldg. C-6841, Fort Bragg, NC 28310; 910-436-1735
82ndairbornedivisionmuseum.com

This museum came on the scene in 1945 as a way to preserve, exhibit, and interpret the history of the 82d Airborne from 1917 to the present day. The self-guided gallery includes original artifacts, plus the museum grounds include captured and used artillery pieces, aircraft, memorials, and other points of interest. Closed Monday, Sunday, January 1, Thanksgiving, and December 25. Free admission; donations appreciated.

3 General William C. Lee Airborne Museum

209 W. Divine St., Dunn, NC 28334; 910-892-1947
generalleeairbornemuseum.org

Major General William C. Lee earned the Distinguished Service Medal for his leadership in airborne forces. He's credited with developing the plans for the air invasion of Normandy on D-Day. He had planned to jump that day, but a heart attack sent him back to North Carolina to his home in Dunn. The museum honoring him is located there today. Closed Sunday, January 1, Martin Luther King Jr. Day, George Washington's Birthday, Memorial Day, July 4, Labor Day, Columbus Day, Veterans Day, Thanksgiving, and December 25. Free admission.

4 Graveyard of the Atlantic Museum

59200 Museum Dr., Hatteras, NC 27943; 252-986-0720
graveyardoftheatlantic.com

Opened in 2002, this museum provides visitors with information on maritime history and shipwrecks of the Outer Banks. Programming—including the Salty Dawg Series, Maritime Crafts, demos of how to make canvas-backed decoys, and other special events—is offered at intervals throughout the year. Closed Sunday, January 1, Martin Luther King Jr. Day, Good Friday, Memorial Day, July 4, Labor Day, Veterans Day, Thanksgiving, day after Thanksgiving, and December 24–26. Free admission.

5 Great Smoky Mountains Railroad

45 Mitchell St., Bryson City, NC 28713; 800-872-4681
gsmr.com

Scenic rail tours depart and return to the historic Bryson City depot. Choices here include a Moonshine Experience, Nantahala Gorge Excursion, and Tuckasegee River Excursion, plus special events like the Polar Express Train and Peanuts The Great Pumpkin Patch Express. January–March, limited weekend trips. April, May, and early November, often closed Sunday and Monday. Closed Thanksgiving and December 25. Check website for train schedule. Admission charged.

6 Hickory Aviation Museum

3101 Ninth Ave. Dr. NW, Hickory, NC 28601; 828-323-1963
hickoryaviationmuseum.org

This museum, located at the Hickory Regional Airport, focuses on presenting aviation history through exhibits and preserved aircraft. Closed Monday, January 1, Easter, Thanksgiving, and December 25. Free admission.

7 National Railroad Museum & Hall of Fame

120 E. Spring St., Hamlet, NC 28345; 910-582-3555
facebook.com/nationalrrmuseumhof

Wives of some Seaboard Air Line Railway workers founded this museum in 1976. Visitors gain a deeper understanding of trains and their historical significance, as well as learn more about the history of Hamlet and Richmond County. Closed Monday–Friday, except by appointment; also closed January 1, Easter, and December 25. Free admission.

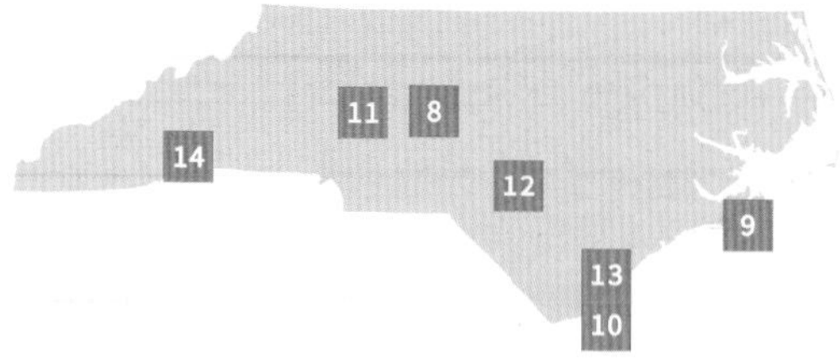

8 North Carolina Aviation Museum & Hall of Fame

2222-G Pilots View Road, Asheboro, NC 27205; 336-625-0170
ncaviationmuseumhalloffame.com

Check out the variety of aircraft here, located at Asheboro Regional Airport. The "infamous Hangar 2" is open for weddings, birthday parties, special events, and photo shoots. Closed Monday–Wednesday, January 1, Easter, Thanksgiving, and December 25. Admission charged.

9 North Carolina Maritime Museum (Beaufort)

315 Front St., Beaufort, NC 28516; 252-504-7740
ncmaritimemuseumbeaufort.com

Interested in Blackbeard? If so, you'll want to see this museum. It serves as the repository for the famed pirate's wrecked flagship, *Queen Anne's Revenge*. The collection includes cannons, belt buckles, and other fascinating artifacts. You can also learn boatbuilding at The Harvey W. Smith Watercraft Center. Check the website for special events and exhibit photos. Closed January 1, Thanksgiving, and December 24–26. Free admission; donations appreciated.

10 North Carolina Maritime Museum (Southport)

204 E. Moore St., Southport, NC 28461; 910-477-5150
ncmaritimemuseumsouthport.com

The exhibits found at the Southport branch of the North Carolina Maritime Museum include information and artifacts relating to the maritime history of the lower Cape Fear River. It provides information and programming on hurricanes, battles, shipwrecks, and more. Closed Sunday and Monday, January 1, Thanksgiving, December 23–26, and December 30–31. Free admission; donations appreciated.

11 North Carolina Transportation Museum

1 Samuel Spencer Dr., Spencer, NC 28159; 704-636-2889
nctrans.org

Artifacts are housed in the remaining building of the Spencer Shops, which served at one time as the largest East Coast repair facility for Southern Railroad's steam locomotives. Among the highlights you'll find the Bob Julian Roundhouse, the largest remaining roundhouse in America. Plan out your visit before going; there are many exhibits and things to discover. Closed Monday, January 1, Easter, Thanksgiving, and December 25; also closed Sundays in January and February. Admission charged.

12 U.S. Army Airborne & Special Operations Museum

100 Bragg Blvd., Fayetteville, NC 28301; 910-643-2778
asomf.org

It first opened on August 16, 2000, to commemorate the 60th anniversary of the first parachute jump conducted by the original Test Platoon. You'll find a main exhibit gallery that presents a self-guided tour of the history from 1940 to present day, a temporary gallery, a theater, and a motion simulator ride (fee charged). It's owned and operated by the U.S. Army. Closed Monday, January 1, Easter, Thanksgiving, and December 25. Free admission.

13 U.S.S. *Battleship North Carolina* Memorial

1 Battleship Road, Wilmington, NC 28401; 910-399-9100
battleshipnc.com

It's easy to spot the ship from downtown Wilmington, but it's even more thrilling to walk its decks and inspect the living quarters and other areas down below. This ship had a stellar career in World War II, earning it 15 battle stars. The ship has been in its current berth in Wilmington since 1961 and was dedicated as a memorial in 1962. Open daily. Admission charged.

14 Western North Carolina Air Museum

1340 Gilbert St., Hendersonville, NC 28793; 828-698-2482
westernnorthcarolinaairmuseum.com

Founded in 1989, this air museum features a variety of historical planes, including a 1917 SE-5A replica, 1915 Nieuport 11 replica, 1932 E-2 Taylor Cub, and others. The museum had a temporary home until a permanent museum hangar was completed in January 1993 adjacent to the Hendersonville Airport. Work on additional hangars began

in 2000. You might be lucky enough to see an owner taking a plane up in the air. Closed Monday–Tuesday, Thursday–Friday, January 1, Easter, Memorial Day, July 4, and December 25. Free admission; donations appreciated.

15 Wilmington Railroad Museum

505 Nutt St., Wilmington, NC 28401; 910-763-2634
wrrm.org

The history of the Atlantic Coast Line Railroad is the focus here. Exhibits include a life-size caboose, a boxcar, a steam locomotive, more than 20 operating model trains, information about famous people involved with railroads—Thomas Edison and George Pullman are two—and the history of railroad development in Wilmington. Kids love the Thomas the Tank Engine play area. Closed Sunday, January 1, Thanksgiving, December 24–25, and December 31. Admission charged.

16 Wright Brothers National Memorial

1000 N. Croatan Hwy., Kill Devil Hills, NC 27948; 252-473-2111
nps.gov/wrbr

It's thrilling to visit the spot where Wilbur and Orville Wright had their first successful airplane flights in 1903. One plaque on the site lists the time of their fourth flight as 59 seconds, in which they traveled 852 feet. Explore the exhibits in the Visitor Center and walk up to the Wright Brothers Monument. Closed December 25. Admission charged.

Learn what it was like for World War II soldiers on the U.S.S. *Battleship North Carolina*.

At Sarah P. Duke Gardens, relax by the Virtue Peace Pond in the Doris Duke Center Gardens.

NORTH CAROLINA'S NATURAL BEAUTY encompasses a diverse assortment of native plants, trees, shrubs, and annual blooms. From the mountains to the coast, there are many prominent gardens where you can explore and appreciate the vast variety—from perennials to orchids to colorful azaleas and rhododendron bushes.

SPEND TIME OUTDOORS:

Gardens, Flowers, & Arboretums

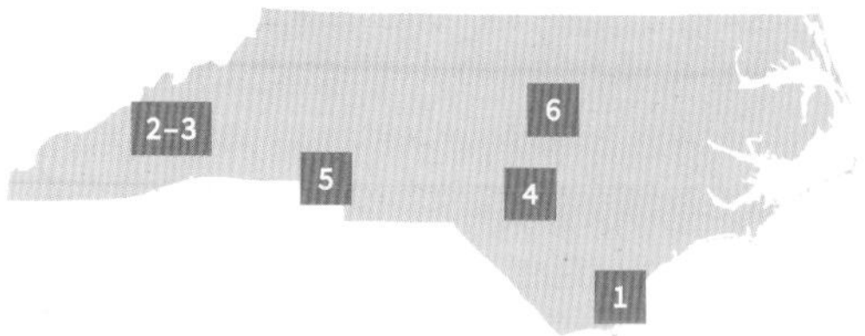

1 Airlie Gardens

300 Airlie Road, Wilmington, NC 28403; 910-798-7700
airliegardens.org

These impressive gardens span across 67 acres with plenty of walking trails to get a closer look. Spring is extraordinary here with more than 75,000 azalea bushes blooming mid-March to mid-April, plus more than 100,000 planted bulbs. Be on the lookout for outdoor sculptures and special treasures like the Bottle Chapel (one of my favorites). A Butterfly House is open May 15–October 15. Closed Mondays January–February; also closed January 1, Thanksgiving, and December 24–25. Admission charged.

2 Biltmore Estate Gardens

1 Lodge St., Asheville, NC 28803; 800-411-3812
biltmore.com

Each season presents unique treasures in the Biltmore estate gardens and grounds. Among the highlights—hundreds of tulips in the Walled Garden, Estate Entry and Winery beds and the impressive azalea gardens in spring, a rose garden with more than 250 varieties, native rhododendrons and perennials from June to August, and the magnificent fall foliage. Open daily. Garden tours are included in the price of Biltmore admission.

3 Botanical Gardens at Asheville

151 W.T. Weaver Blvd., Asheville, NC 28804-3414; 828-252-5190
ashevillebotanicalgardens.org

This 10-acre site, adjacent to the campus of the University of North Carolina at Asheville, is a fun place to take a stroll and soak in the peace and solitude. Most of the blooms appear between mid-April to mid-August. Trees and plants are identified with name markers. One trail leads to a historical dogtrot cabin. Open daily, dawn–dusk. Free admission; donations appreciated.

4 Cape Fear Botanical Garden

536 N. Eastern Blvd., Fayetteville, NC 28301; 910-486-0221
capefearbg.org

This garden serves as a North Carolina Environmental Education Center and as an approved Cumberland County Field Trip Destination. Tours are available year-round, but the peak season for blooms is March–October. Families with kids will want to check out a backpack to participate in a scavenger hunt and make sure to explore the Children's Garden and Butterfly Stroll. Standard wheelchairs can travel most of the paths, and those with disabilities may also reserve a golf cart to travel around the garden; the rental fee includes a garden-provided driver. Closed January 1, Thanksgiving, and December 24–25. Admission charged.

5 Daniel Stowe Botanical Garden

6500 S. New Hope Road, Belmont, NC 28012; 704-825-4490
dsbg.org

The vision of retired textile executive Daniel Jonathan Stowe resulted in this garden. In 1991 he set aside almost 400 acres of land for the garden's creation. Three years later a master plan was created to cultivate the property over a period of 50 years. In 1999 the Visitor Pavilion, Formal Display Gardens, and Perennial Gardens opened, followed by the White Garden in 2003, the Orchid Conservatory in 2008, the children's garden in 2014, and the Dry Piedmont Prairie Garden in 2019. The glass conservatory contains 8,000 square feet over five stories and hosts a gorgeous display of orchids and tropical plants. Special events are held throughout the year. Closed Thanksgiving and December 25. Admission charged.

6 Dr. Martin Luther King, Jr. Memorial Gardens

1215 Martin Luther King Jr. Blvd., Raleigh, NC 27610; 919-996-3285
raleighnc.gov/parks/content/ParksRec/Articles/Parks/MLKGardens.html

Created in 1975, this 2.4-acre site is the country's first public park dedicated only to honoring Dr. Martin Luther King Jr. and the civil rights movement. A highlight is a sculpture of King—a 6-foot, 2-inch piece of bronze fashioned by Abbe Godwin. A striking water monument honors other pioneers of the civil rights movement. Open daily, dawn–dusk. Free admission.

7 JC Raulston Arboretum

4415 Beryl Road, Raleigh, NC 27606; 919-515-3132
jcra.ncsu.edu

This arboretum is named for the late J. C. Raulston, a former professor who taught in the Department of Horticultural Science at North Carolina State University and who was instrumental in its creation. It showcases a large and diverse collection of plants through multiple gardens. Grounds open daily, dawn–dusk. Buildings open fewer hours and closed January 1, Martin Luther King Jr. Day, Good Friday, Memorial Day, July 4, Labor Day, Veterans Day, Thanksgiving, day after Thanksgiving, and December 24–26. Free admission; donations appreciated.

8 Juniper Level Botanic Garden

9241 Sauls Road, Raleigh, NC 27603; 919-772-4794
jlbg.org

These gardens, which cover more than 25 acres, were founded in 1988 by Tony and Michelle Avent. The site is only open eight weekends a year. However, guests may also schedule an appointment to visit at other times by filling out a visit request form on the website. Native, rare, and unique perennials are a special focus here. Free admission, but appointments are required most of the year.

9 The North Carolina Arboretum

100 Frederick Law Olmsted Way, Asheville, NC 28806; 828-665-2492
ncarboretum.org

This 434-acre public garden makes its home within the Bent Creek Experimental Forest near the Blue Ridge Parkway. It offers many opportunities to explore, with carefully manicured gardens and hiking and mountain biking trails. The arboretum also hosts a variety of special exhibits and events. Winter Lights, held during the holiday season, features unique displays using more than 500,000 holiday lights (admission charged). Open daily. Free admission, but a parking fee is charged.

10 North Carolina Botanical Garden and Coker Arboretum

100 Old Mason Farm Road, Chapel Hill, NC 27517; 919-962-0522
ncbg.unc.edu/coker-arboretum

This garden's beginnings date back to 1903 when Dr. William Chambers Coker, the University of North Carolina's first botany professor, began making an outdoor classroom for his students to have access to native plants, trees, and shrubs. It grew over time and now includes beauty in every season. Coker Arboretum is located beside the Morehead Planetarium & Science Center. Free hour-long tours are offered the third Saturday of each month, March–November. Open daily, dawn–dusk. Free admission; donations appreciated.

11 Raleigh Rose Garden

301 Pogue St., Raleigh, NC 27607; 919-821-4579 or 919-996-4810
raleighlittletheatre.org/visit-us/rose-garden

Savor the smell of roses here, where 60 varieties of roses bloom from late May until fall. Concerts and special events are staged at an amphitheater in the garden, which is part of the Raleigh Little Theatre campus. Open daily, dawn–dusk. Free admission.

12 Reynolda Gardens of Wake Forest University

100 Reynolda Village, Winston-Salem, NC 27106; 336-758-5593
reynoldagardens.org

Reynolda is the former home of tobacco magnate R. J. Reynolds and his wife, Katharine Smith Reynolds. The Reynolda Gardens comprise 129 acres and include formal gardens, a conservatory, and working greenhouses. Open daily, dawn–dusk. The greenhouses are closed on Sunday, on Saturday in January and July, and during the Wake University winter holiday. Free admission.

13 Sarah P. Duke Gardens

420 Anderson St., Durham, NC 27705; 919-684-3698
gardens.duke.edu

Founded in 1934, these 55-acre gardens have won multiple awards and honors, including being consistently ranked Durham's #1 attraction by TripAdvisor. Four distinct gardens are featured: the Historic Gardens, H. L. Blomquist Garden of Native Plants, William Louis Culberson Asiatic Arboretum, and Doris Duke Center & Gardens. Guided walking tours and trolley tours are offered at specific days and times; fee charged. Open daily, 8 a.m.–dusk. Free admission, but parking fee charged.

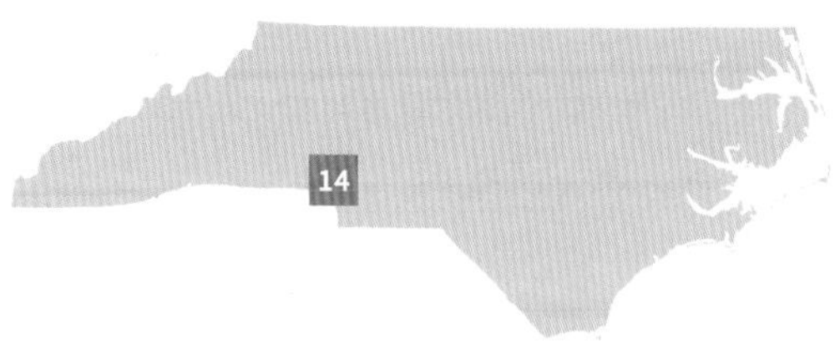

14 UNC Charlotte Botanical Gardens

9090 Craver Road, Charlotte, NC 28262; 704-687-0721
gardens.uncc.edu

Established in 1966 as a living classroom for students, this site has expanded over the years to encompass 10 acres of outdoor gardens, a glasshouse with workspace, and a teaching classroom that includes a botanical and horticultural library. The website details when certain plants peak throughout the year. Grounds open daily, dawn–dusk. Free admission.

Azaleas bloom in spring at Biltmore Estate.
(photographed by Maria Milling)

Cross the Mile High Swinging Bridge on Grandfather Mountain for spectacular views.

OF ALL THE DAY-TRIP POSSIBILITIES in this book, I believe these incredible natural wonders are the top places to visit. The natural beauty in North Carolina is often mind-boggling. Make a checklist and see how many of these places you can find time to explore.

SPEND TIME OUTDOORS:

Natural Wonders

1 The Blowing Rock

432 The Rock Road, Blowing Rock, NC 28605; 828-295-7111
theblowingrock.com

It's estimated that The Blowing Rock, comprised of gneiss, formed 1.055 billion years ago. Several American Indian legends and stories are associated with this place, which even got the attention of *Ripley's Believe It or Not!*, which dubbed it the "only place in the world where snow falls upside down." January–March, closed Tuesday–Wednesday; April–December, open daily; weather permitting. Admission charged.

2 Chimney Rock State Park

431 Main St., Chimney Rock, NC 28720; 828-625-9611
chimneyrockpark.com or ncparks.gov/chimney-rock-state-park

Dr. Lucius B. Morse was one of many who came to Western North Carolina to seek a healthful climate after being diagnosed with tuberculosis. The Chimney Rock area, including the towering monolith, inspired him so much that he bought it. He paid a mere $5,000 for 64 acres in 1902. Land has been accumulated over the years to expand the park to almost 1,000 acres. You can walk to the top of the Chimney or ride an elevator. Closed Thanksgiving and December 25; open daily, weather permitting. Admission charged.

3 French Broad River

blueridgeheritage.com/destinations/french-broad-river

The mighty French Broad River rambles about 70 miles as it flows through Western North Carolina into Tennessee. It's popular for tubing, whitewater rafting, canoeing, kayaking, and fishing.

4 Grandfather Mountain

2050 Blowing Rock Hwy., Linville, NC 28646; 800-468-7325
grandfather.com

Cherokee Indians called this place Tanawha, which means "a fabulous hawk or eagle." Settlers, however, called it Grandfather because they could see the profile of an old man jutting up toward the sky.

The stunning scenic beauty is complemented by a man-made design: the Mile High Swinging Bridge, created in 1952. Closed Thanksgiving and December 25; open daily, weather permitting. Admission charged.

5 Jockey's Ridge State Park

300 W. Carolista Dr., Nags Head, NC 27959; 252-441-7132
ncparks.gov/jockeys-ridge-state-park

It's estimated that the sand dunes here formed 3,000–4,000 years ago. Wind blows through the dunes to create new patterns in the ridgeline, with some dunes rising as high as 60 feet. Because of this constant change, Jockey's Ridge is often called a living dune. The dunes cover 426 acres. Closed December 25. Free admission.

6 Lake Mattamuskeet

85 Mattamuskeet Road, Swan Quarter, NC 27885; 252-926-4021
fws.gov/refuge/mattamuskeet

At 18 miles long and 7 miles wide, Lake Mattamuskeet's claim to fame is that of North Carolina's largest natural lake. It's also pretty shallow—2–3 feet in most places. It's the largest part of the Mattamuskeet National Wildlife Refuge.

7 Linville Caverns

19929 US 221 N, Marion, NC 28752; 800-419-0540
linvillecaverns.com

A fishing expedition led by Henry Colton discovered the caverns in the early 1800s. They investigated after seeing fish swimming into the mountain. The caverns first opened to the public in 1937. Tours continue today to offer a look at this subterranean world. Make sure to take a sweatshirt or jacket with you—the caverns here stay a cool 52° year-round. January, February, and December, open Saturday–Sunday only; March–November, open daily. Admission charged.

8 Looking Glass Rock

FS 475, 0.5 mile west of US 276, Brevard, NC 28712; 828-877-3265
tinyurl.com/pisgahlookingglass

This domed mountaintop is stunning from a distance, but it's also a wonderful place to enjoy the natural environment. The Looking Glass Rock Trail to the summit climbs 1,600 feet and provides incredible views. There's need for caution here—a steep, sharp drop from the top has resulted in tragic falls in the past.

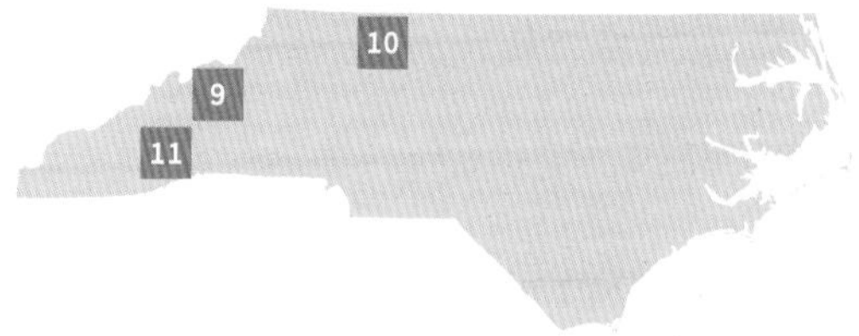

9 Mount Mitchell State Park

2388 NC 128, Burnsville, NC 28714; 828-675-4611
ncparks.gov/mount-mitchell-state-park

Mount Mitchell rises to a height of 6,684 feet, making it the highest point east of the Mississippi River. Learn about the history of the area in the on-site museum (open May–October) and enjoy the natural beauty and opportunities for hiking, camping, and backpacking. Closed December 25. Free admission.

10 Pilot Mountain State Park

1792 Pilot Knob Park Road, Pinnacle, NC 27043; 336-325-2355
ncparks.gov/pilot-mountain-state-park

This striking mountain, rising more than 2,000 feet, has long served as an area landmark. Rock climbing and rappelling are permitted on some of the cliffs. Other activities include canoeing, hiking, camping, and horseback riding. Closed December 25. Free admission.

11 Sliding Rock

US 276, 7.2 miles south of the Blue Ridge Pkwy., Pisgah Forest, NC 28768;
828-885-7625
tinyurl.com/slidingrockrecarea

Sliding Rock is just what it sounds like—a big natural rock used as a fun slide into an 8-foot pool of water. Open year-round, but lifeguards and open restrooms are only available Memorial Day–Labor Day and intermittently through mid-October. Fee charged.

Looking Glass Rock stands out from the surrounding Pisgah National Forest.

Hanging Rock State Park provides many opportunities for outdoor enthusiasts.

NORTH CAROLINA'S UNIQUE LOCATION covering mountains to sea offers a broad, extensive range of outdoor adventures. Whether you're careening over rushing whitewater in a raft, kayak, or canoe; boating in the ocean; fishing in a stream; pedaling a mountain bike up a steep trail; hiking to the top of a summit; or climbing a rock face, there's an abundance of places to explore. You'll find everything from easy, mild activities to extreme adventures that put your skills and courage to the test.

SPEND TIME OUTDOORS:

Outdoor Adventures

Joyce Kilmer Memorial Forest brings Kilmer's poem "Trees" to life.

1 Appalachian Trail

appalachiantrail.org; 304-535-6331

It takes months for thru-hikers to complete the entire Appalachian Trail, which runs almost 2,200 miles from Springer Mountain in Georgia to Mount Katahdin in Maine. North Carolina contains almost 96 miles of the trail, with an additional 225 miles running along the Tennessee–North Carolina border. Day hikers can do section hikes of the AT.

2 Blue Ridge Parkway

nps.gov/blri; 828-348-3400

This ribbon of road runs from Cherokee, North Carolina, to the Skyline Drive in Virginia. The last time I took a trip on a major stretch of the parkway, I counted no fewer than 11 deer. I spotted each one randomly at different intervals along the drive. The speed limit is 45 (35 in some spots), so it's not a fast journey. Overlooks and pull-offs provide opportunities to explore hiking trails and points of interest.

3 Great Smoky Mountains National Park

nps.gov/grsm; 865-436-1200

This very popular national park is located in portions of Western North Carolina and East Tennessee. The North Carolina side offers a myriad of hiking trails, fishing and boating at Fontana Dam, bicycling, camping, and picnicking, as well as chances to see the reintroduced elk herd at Cataloochee Valley. Free admission.

4 Hanging Rock State Park

1790 Hanging Rock Park Road, Danbury, NC 27016; 336-593-8480
ncparks.gov/hanging-rock-state-park

The Civilian Conservation Corps (CCC) developed this park in the 1930s. It features 20 miles of hiking trails, 8 miles of mountain biking trails, rock climbing opportunities (requires a free permit), and a 73-site campground. The park also offers canoeing and swimming activities and free interpretative programs. Closed December 25. Free admission.

5 Joyce Kilmer Memorial Forest

5410 Joyce Kilmer Road, Robbinsville, NC 28771; 828-479-6431
tinyurl.com/joycekilmermf

Located near Robbinsville, this 3,800-acre forest serves as a memorial to Joyce Kilmer, best known for writing the poem "Trees." Kilmer was killed by a sniper in France during World War I. This memorial forest is located within the Joyce Kilmer–Slickrock Wilderness Area, which contains more than 17,000 acres. Hiking is a popular activity in this old-growth forest.

6 Linville Gorge Wilderness

tinyurl.com/linvillegorgewild; 828-652-2144

Located within the Pisgah National Forest, this wilderness area offers hiking, backpacking, rock climbing, fishing, hunting, and camping. A free camping permit is required for weekends and holidays May–October. Reservations are first-come, first-serve and fill up quickly. Reserve a permit by calling the Grandfather Ranger District at 828-652-2144.

7 Masonboro Island Reserve

GPS coordinates: N34° 07.989' W77° 51.063'; 910-962-2998
nccoastalreserve.net/web/crp/masonboro-island

Masonboro Island is a delight for the senses because you won't find any streetlights, cars, hotels, or any sign of modern-day commercialism. It's the largest undisturbed barrier island along North Carolina's southern coast and serves as a dedicated nature preserve. Primitive camping is allowed here, but care must be taken not to disturb fragile habitat areas. The island can only be reached by boat. I highly recommend Wrightsville Beach Scenic Tours (wrightsvillebeachscenictours.com), owned by Captain Joe Abbate.

8 Mountains-to-Sea Trail

mountainstoseatrail.org; 919-825-0297

Explore the state by foot. You can literally hike all the way from the mountains to the sea. The Mountains-to-Sea Trail stretches from Clingmans Dome in the Great Smoky Mountains National Park to Jockey's Ridge on the Outer Banks. There are 18 trail segments and one alternate route. An interactive map on the website will alert you to any detours if portions of the trail are closed.

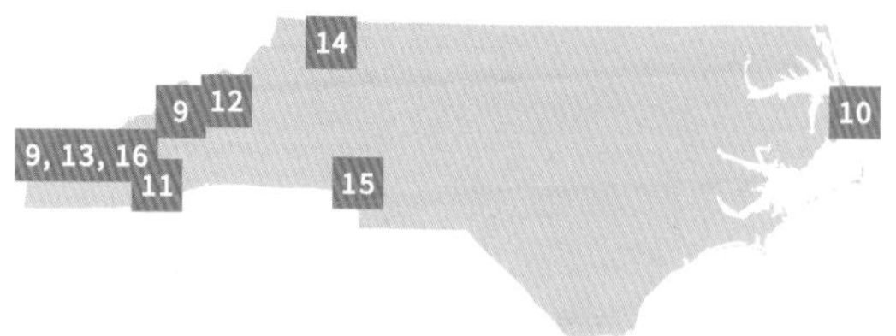

9 Nantahala Outdoor Center

Nantahala location: 13077 US 19 W, Bryson City, NC 28713
French Broad location: 9825 US 25 Marshall, NC 28753
noc.com; 828-785-4846

Ready to test your skills in the water? The Nantahala Outdoor Center offers many opportunities here, including a chance to attend paddling school to learn new skills or advance to the next level. Learn white-water kayaking or canoeing, or if you're ready for a new career, go to raft guide school. Beyond the schooling, choose from whitewater trips, zip lines, and a River-to-Ridge rafting plus zip line package.

10 Outer Banks

1 Visitors Center Cir., Manteo, NC 27954; 877-629-4386
outerbanks.org

The Outer Banks are a string of barrier islands off the coast of North Carolina—200 miles in length. Outdoor adventures here cover a wide range of activities: fishing, swimming, surfing, kayaking, windsurfing, bird-watching, golfing, biking, and off-road driving.

11 Panthertown Valley

panthertown.org or tinyurl.com/panthertown; 828-269-4453 or 828-524-6441

Panthertown Valley, located within the Nantahala National Forest, is part of a 10,000-acre tract of protected public land. The Panthertown Valley area is comprised of 6,295 acres and offers 30 miles of back-country trails popular for hiking, rock climbing, camping, mountain biking, and horseback riding (the latter two on designated trails).

12 Pisgah National Forest

tinyurl.com/pisgahnf; 828-257-4200

George Vanderbilt, who built Biltmore Estate in Asheville, once owned a large portion of what is now the Pisgah National Forest (PNF). After his death, his wife, Edith, sold a large portion of the estate to the federal government for the purpose of establishing PNF. The Cradle of Forestry is located within its boundaries. There are places to camp, fish, hike, picnic, mountain bike, and take part in other activities. For specific information visit the website above and look for a link to the camping and day-use guide.

13 Shining Rock Wilderness

tinyurl.com/shiningrock; 828-877-3265

Located north of the Blue Ridge Parkway, this 18,000-acre wilderness area is found between US 276 and NC 215. As a federally designated wilderness area, specific rules strive to minimize habitat damage. Trails are not signed, campfires are not allowed, bicycles are not allowed, and groups must include fewer than 10 people.

14 Stone Mountain State Park

3042 Frank Pkwy., Roaring Gap, NC 28668; 336-957-8185
ncparks.gov/stone-mountain-state-park

The focal point here is a massive granite dome known as Stone Mountain. The area hosts all types of outdoor adventures: camping, hiking, horseback riding, fishing, and more. The area includes a 90-site campground, more than 18 miles of trails, and more than 20 miles of designated trout waters. Permits are required for rock climbing on the 600-foot granite face. Closed December 25. Free admission.

15 U.S. National Whitewater Center

5000 Whitewater Center Pkwy., Charlotte, NC 28214; 704-391-3900
usnwc.org

Get ready to play hard here. More than 1,300 acres are filled with outdoor adventure opportunities, such as whitewater rafting, kayaking, mountain biking, trail running, zip lines, stand-up paddleboarding, marathons, triathlons, and more. Closed Thanksgiving and December 25. Pass purchases include day passes, annual passes, and single activity passes. Guided tours include a canopy tour, a zip line tour, and a raft plus zip line tour.

16 Western North Carolina Fly Fishing Trail

flyfishingtrail.com; 800-962-1911

Follow the trail to 15 of the best spots in Western North Carolina to catch brook, brown, and rainbow trout. Jackson County has more than 4,600 miles of trout streams, giving you plenty of opportunities to catch the big one. The largest recorded rainbow trout in North Carolina was caught in this county. Download a trail map online, which includes GPS coordinates for each spot.

Enjoying the Snow

DOWNHILL SKIING

Appalachian Ski Mtn.
940 Ski Mountain Road, Blowing Rock, NC 28605; 828-295-7828; appskimtn.com

Beech Mountain Resort
1007 Beech Mountain Pkwy., Beech Mountain, NC 28604; 828-387-2011
beechmountainresort.com

Cataloochee Ski Area
1080 Ski Lodge Road, Maggie Valley, NC 28751; 828-926-0285; cataloochee.com

Sapphire Valley Ski Area
127 Cherokee Trail, Sapphire Valley, NC 28774; 828-743-7663; skisapphirevalley.com

Sugar Mountain Resort
1009 Sugar Mountain Dr., Sugar Mountain, NC 28604; 828-898-4521; skisugar.com

Wolf Ridge Ski Resort
578 Valley View Cir., Mars Hill, NC 28754; 828-689-4111; skiwolfridgenc.com

SNOW TUBING

Beech Mountain Resort Tubing
1007 Beech Mountain Pkwy., Beech Mountain, NC 28604; 828-387-2011
beechmountainresort.com/mountain/tubing

Black Bear Snow Tubing
373 Kerr Road, Hendersonville, NC 28792; 828-685-1155; blackbearsnowtubing.com

Cataloochee Tube World
1080 Ski Lodge Road, Maggie Valley, NC 28751; 828-926-0285
cataloochee.com/planning/tube-world

Hawksnest Snow Tubing Park
2058 Skyland Dr., Seven Devils, NC 28604; 828-963-6561; hawksnesttubing.com

Jonas Ridge Snow Tubing
9472 NC 181 S, Jonas Ridge, NC 28641; 828-733-4155; jonasridgesnowtube.com

Moonshine Mountain Snow Tubing Park
5865 Willow Road, Hendersonville, NC 28739; 828-689-0333
moonshinemountain.com

Sugar Mountain Resort Tubing
1009 Sugar Mountain Dr., Sugar Mountain, NC 28604; 828-898-4521
skisugar.com/tubing

Zip-n-Slip Snow Tubing
10725 US 23, Mars Hill, NC 28754; 828-689-8444; zipnslip.com

Above the Ground

SKYDIVING

Skydive Central North Carolina
4235 Pool View Dr., Maiden, NC 28650; 704-787-5944; skydivecentralnc.com

Skydive Paraclete XP
143 Airport Dr., Raeford, NC 28376; 910-904-0000; skydiveparacletexp.com

ZIP-LINING

The Adventure Center of Asheville
85 Expo Dr., Asheville, NC 28806; 877-247-5539; ashevilletreetopsadventurepark.com

Beanstalk Ziplines
701 Sanford Dr., Morganton, NC 28655; 828-430-3440; thebeanstalkjourney.com

Nantahala Outdoor Center Mountaintop Zip Line Tour
13077 US 19 W, Bryson City, NC 28713; 828-785-5557; noc.com

Navitat
242 Poverty Branch Road, Barnardsville, NC 28709; 828-626-3700
navitat.com/asheville-nc

Richland Creek Zip Line Canopy Tour
2728 Fairview Farms, Asheboro, NC 27205; 336-736-5623; richlandcreekzipline.com

Find your own treasures at one of the state's many gem mines.
(photographed by Marla Milling)

GEM MINING qualifies as one of the most relaxing activities I've ever experienced. Getting your hands in the dirt provides a calming connection to the earth. It's also comforting in the way it forces you to focus on the present moment as you scan for treasures. Two areas of Western North Carolina are especially rich with gemstones and minerals: Mitchell County (namely Spruce Pine) and Macon County (Franklin), which is known as the Gem Capital of the World. Best tips: Wear shoes you don't mind getting muddy, old clothes, and sunscreen, though many flumes are covered.

SPEND TIME OUTDOORS:

Rocks & Minerals

This old steam engine was used to transport ore at the Bon Ami Mine. You can see it at the North Carolina Mining Museum.

1 Aurora Fossil Museum

400 Main St., Aurora, NC 27806; 252-322-4238
aurorafossilmuseum.org

This museum showcases a wide variety of Miocene and Pliocene marine fossils and specimens from the neighboring Nutrien Phosphate Mine. Also on display are a world-class array of gems and minerals, including a fluorescent mineral room and fossils from around the world (the remnants of an Ice Age mastodon are in the mix). A fun aspect of this museum is Fossil Park, where visitors can dig for their own fossils. It's located across the street from the main entrance. Bring your own trowel, sifter, and bags to carry your finds home. Closed January 1, Easter, Thanksgiving, and December 24–25. Free admission; donations appreciated.

2 Cherokee Ruby and Sapphire Mine

41 Cherokee Mine Road, Franklin, NC 28734; 828-349-2941
cherokeerubymine.com

Billed as Macon County's only 100% unsalted gem mine, this mine has produced the extremely rare star rubies, star sapphires, and star garnets, as well as a mixture of other gems native to the area. Open May–October, daily, weather permitting; see website for closed dates. No admission after 1 p.m. Fees charged by the bucket.

3 Crystal Mountain Gem Mine

31 S. Broad St., Brevard, NC 28712; 828-877-4700
crystalmarketminingcompany.com

Emeralds, sapphires, and rubies are among the possible stones you'll find at this gem mine. One unique feature is the 52-foot-long indoor water flume. There's also a well-stocked rock and fossil shop. Closed December 25. Fees charged by the bucket.

4 Doc's Rocks Gem Mine

111 Mystery Hill Lane, Blowing Rock, NC 28605; 828-264-4499
docsrocks.org

Billed as "North Carolina's premier geology education center," this facility offers special summer trips and rock hound tours at a variety of locations. Owner Randy "Doc" McCoy opened the place in 2007. He double majored in geology and recreation management at nearby Appalachian State University. He cuts gemstones and sells more than 100,000 different varieties in his store. Closed December 24–25. Fees charged by the bucket.

5 Elijah Mountain Gem Mining

2120 Brevard Road, Hendersonville, NC 28739; 828-692-6560
elijahmountain.com

This place offers covered outdoor flumes, indoor flumes, and wheelchair access to mining. The buckets are salted with a variety of gemstones to discover—more than 40 types of gems are possible in every bucket. Gemstone cutting, as well as identification of the stones you've found, is available on-site. Family owned and operated. Closed Easter, Thanksgiving, and December 25. Fees charged by the bucket.

6 Emerald Hollow Mine

484 Emerald Hollow Mine Dr., Hiddenite, NC 28636; 828-635-7548
emeraldhollowmine.com

This is an active mine, so visitors must purchase a permit to take part in three main activities: sluicing, creeking, and digging. Sluicing involves sitting at the covered sluiceway and washing/sorting through buckets of dirt in hopes of finding a treasure. Creeking involves using a plastic trowel to dig and then filter the dirt through a sifting screen. More than 60 different types of naturally occurring gemstones and minerals have been discovered here. They also have a full-service lapidary shop to transform your rough stones into a beautifully cut piece of jewelry. Closed Thanksgiving and December 24–25. Fees charged by the bucket.

7 Emerald Village and North Carolina Mining Museum

331 McKinney Mine Road, Spruce Pine, NC 28777; 828-765-6463
emeraldvillage.com

The North Carolina Mining Museum at Emerald Village allows participants a chance to go underground into the historic Bon Ami mine. The mine opened in 1924 to retrieve feldspar used in production of Bon Ami

scouring cleanser. Black light mine tours are offered on select dates throughout the year—under the ultraviolet light deposits of hyalite opal glow a vivid lime green and feldspar glows pink to red. You can also sift through salted gemstone buckets at Emerald Village or drive to the nearby Crabtree Emerald Mine and spend a day using hand tools to dig for emeralds. Open late March–November. Admission charged at museum; fees charged by the bucket at the mine.

8 Franklin Gem & Mineral Museum

25 Phillips St., Franklin, NC 28734; 828-369-7831
fgmm.org

One of the largest collections of gems and minerals in the Southeast is housed in the old jail building in Franklin. Eight rooms are filled with specimens from around the world. Franklin is located in Macon County, which is known as the Gem Capital of the World, for its abundance of quartz, garnets, rubies, and other gemstones. There's also a gift shop. Open May–October, Monday–Saturday; November–April, Saturday only. Free admission; donations appreciated.

9 Gold City Gem Mine

9410 Sylva Road, Franklin, NC 28734; 800-713-7767
goldcityamusement.com

A 10-year-old boy found a real treasure in this mine in 1995. He was working through a $10 bucket of dirt at the flume when he found an interesting rock. It turned out to be a sapphire weighing in at a whopping 1,061 carats. The covered flume makes it easy to search for gemstones in any weather; in winter they have an indoor flume. Closed Monday. Fees charged by the bucket.

10 Jackson Hole Trading Post & Gem Mine

9770 Highlands Road, Highlands, NC 28741; 828-524-5850
jacksonholegemmine.com

You'll find native and enriched gemstones here. If you find a stone that you want set in a piece of jewelry, they offer services to transform it for you. Located near some beautiful waterfalls, this mine is 0.3 mile from Cullasaja Falls and 5 miles from Dry Falls. Hours vary, so call or check the website before you go. Fees charged by the bucket.

11 The Learning Center at PARI

1 PARI Dr., Rosman, NC 28772; 828-862-5554
pari.edu

The Learning Center at PARI (Pisgah Astronomical Research Institute) offers a unique chance to see a collection of gems, minerals, and meteorites. The Exhibit Gallery includes pieces of rare meteorites, samples taken from Mars and the moon, and a one-third-scale Apollo 11 Lunar Module model. The collection also includes other gems found in North Carolina: rubies, sapphires, garnets, amethysts, and more. Hours vary, so call or check the website before you go. Admission charged.

12 Mineral and Lapidary Museum of Henderson County

400 N. Main St., Hendersonville, NC 28792; 828-698-1977
mineralmuseum.org

Volunteers run this museum and are eager to share their knowledge of the exhibits. Holdings here include a large collection of geodes, specimens of raw minerals in their natural state, polished gemstones, and a collection of fossils, including the leg bone of a woolly mammoth. The gift shop features a wide array of jewelry, as well as minerals, fossils, tumbled stones, and posters. Closed Sunday, January–February, Thanksgiving, and December 24–25. Free admission; donations appreciated.

13 Museum of North Carolina Minerals

79 Parkway Maintenance Road, Spruce Pine, NC 28777; 828-765-2761
nps.gov/blri/planyourvisit/museum-of-north-carolina-minerals-mp-331.htm

The Museum of North Carolina Minerals, located just off the Blue Ridge Parkway in Spruce Pine, is situated in an area prominent for its wealth of minerals and gems. This museum features interactive displays about the minerals and gems found in the region and also provides insight into the historical importance of the mining industry to the economic health of the area. It's located at Gillespie Gap, which served as a vital stop for Revolutionary War soldiers traveling to the Battle of Kings Mountain. The museum hosts a reenactment of the Overmountain Men each September. Open daily. Free admission.

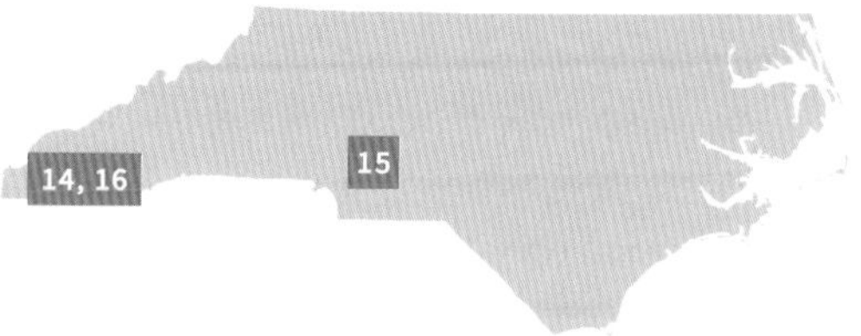

14 Old Cardinal Gem Mine

71 Rockhaven Dr., Franklin, NC 28734; 828-524-7306
oldcardinalgemmine.com

There's a choice here: purchase a bucket of prefilled dirt or dig your own. Sift the dirt and see what rocks you find at the bottom of the screen. This mine has a 40-year history of producing sapphires, garnets, rubies, amethysts, and moonstones. Open Sunday–Friday; by appointment only on Saturday. Fees charged by the bucket.

15 Reed Gold Mine

9621 Reed Mine Road, Midland, NC 28107; 704-721-4653
historicsites.nc.gov/all-sites/reed-gold-mine

Here's an interesting tidbit about North Carolina history—the first documented gold find in the country was discovered at the site of the Reed Gold Mine in Midland. North Carolina actually led the nation in gold production until 1948, when the California gold rush took center stage. Gold panning is offered April–October. Guided tours of the underground tunnels are offered November–March, and the rest of the year, you can take a self-guided tour of the stamp mill and underground tunnels. The visitor center features exhibits about the geology of gold, the history of gold mining in the state, and information about the Reed family. Closed Sunday, Monday, January 1, Good Friday, July 4, Thanksgiving, day after Thanksgiving, and December 24–25. Free admission, but fees charged for gold panning.

16 Rose Creek Mine

115 Terrace Ridge Dr., Franklin, NC 28734; 828-349-3774
rosecreekmine.com

Dig your own bucket of dirt in the mining tunnel and then sift it at the covered flume. This mine is one of three state-licensed gem mines operating in Macon County. Gems found here include rubies, sapphires, smoky quartz, topaz, moonstones, citrines, garnets, and amethysts. It has a rock and gift shop offering jewelry, lapidary supplies, and gem dirt to go. Open April–October; closed Sunday and some Wednesdays. Fees charged by the bucket.

Explore Reed Gold Mine, where gold was first discovered in the United States.

DuPont State Recreational Forest contains many waterfalls, including Triple Falls. (photographed by Bill Russ/Distl PR)

IT WOULD BE IMPOSSIBLE to detail all of the beautiful waterfalls located in North Carolina. Transylvania County alone has more than 250 of these natural wonders! That area is definitely a good starting point for those wanting to experience the beauty of viewing waterfalls in person. With these listings, I also hit the high spots of some of the other waterfalls you'll want to see. A word of warning: Every year there are reports of waterfall accidents. Avoid places near the top of any waterfall, and don't cross behind any warning signs. For other practical safety tips, visit explorebrevard.com/waterfall-safety.

SPEND TIME OUTDOORS:

Waterfalls

1 Bust Your Butt Falls

GPS coordinates: N35° 05.581' W83° 15.953'
highlandschamber.org/play/#!directory

This cascading waterfall, with multiple tiers and a deep pool at the bottom, becomes a popular gathering spot, especially in the summer when people are seeking a fun swimming hole. There's a jump-off rock here, but use caution. Located 6.5 miles west of Highlands and 10 miles south of Franklin on the Cullasaja River along US 64.

2 Catawba Falls

GPS coordinates: N35° 36.832' W82° 13.787'; 828-652-2144
tinyurl.com/catawbawf

A 4-mile round-trip hike leads to these beautiful, cascading waterfalls, located near Old Fort. The U.S. Forest Service upgraded the site in 2012 with the addition of a parking lot and restrooms. There are upper and lower falls with dozens of smaller cascades.

3 Crabtree Falls

Milepost 339.5 on the Blue Ridge Pkwy., Burnsville, NC 28714; 828-348-3400
nps.gov/blri/planyourvisit/crabtree-falls-trail.htm

The 2.5-mile round-trip hike to Crabtree Falls takes up to 2.5 hours, depending on your pace and how much time you spend enjoying the falls. The trail itself is rated moderate to strenuous. You can return the same way you came or head out on a longer, gradual ascent to the parking area.

4 DuPont State Recreational Forest Falls

89 Buck Forest Road, Cedar Mountain, NC 28718; 828-877-6527
dupontstaterecreationalforest.com

The beautiful assortment of waterfalls in this state forest includes Hooker Falls, Bridal Veil Falls, High Falls, Triple Falls, and Grassy Creek Falls. Download a map of the area before heading out—you'll find it on the website.

5 Gorges State Park Falls

976 Grassy Ridge Road, Sapphire, NC 28774; 828-966-9099
ncparks.gov/gorges-state-park

This park, encompassing 7,500 acres, provides access to beautiful waterfalls—Rainbow Falls, Turtleback Falls, Upper Bearwallow Falls, and Lower Bearwallow Falls. Find the trail map on the website and print it before you go. You can also get one at the park office. Closed December 25. Free admission.

6 Hickory Nut Falls

431 Main St., Chimney Rock, NC 28720; 828-625-9611
chimneyrockpark.com or ncparks.gov/chimney-rock-state-park

Located within Chimney Rock State Park, a 0.75-mile trail leads to the bottom of the 404-foot Hickory Nut Falls. It's a bit famous since it served as a backdrop in scenes of *The Last of the Mohicans*. Closed Thanksgiving and December 25; open daily, weather permitting. Admission charged.

7 Land of the Waterfalls

Transylvania County; 828-884-8900
explorebrevard.com/the-great-outdoors/waterfalls

Whitewater Falls—ranked as the highest waterfall east of the Rocky Mountains—is one of the 250 waterfalls found in Transylvania County. Its falls plunge 411 feet. From Brevard, travel west on US 64 almost 18 miles to Sapphire and turn left on NC 281. Travel south 8.5 miles, and turn left to access the trailhead for Whitewater Falls (N35° 01.766' W83° 00.974'). The ever-popular Looking Glass Falls (N35° 17.781' W82° 46.165') with roadside viewing and Sliding Rock (see page 150) are also found in Transylvania County. Get a map and chart out a plan to discover as many as you desire.

8 Linville Falls

Milepost 316.4 on the Blue Ridge Pkwy., Jonas Ridge, NC 28657; 828-348-3400
nps.gov/blri/planyourvisit/linville-falls-mp-316.htm

Follow your choice of two trails to the falls from the visitor center. Five different viewpoints are accessible from these trails. Make sure to take your camera—there's a lot of beauty here—and carve out time to spend a full day exploring the area, hiking, and picnicking. The Linville Falls area is accessed between mileposts 316 and 317 along the Blue Ridge Parkway.

9 Mingo Falls

71 Big Cove Road, Cherokee, NC 28719; 865-436-1200
nps.gov/grsm/planyourvisit/mingo-falls.htm

Mingo Falls, at 120 feet, is one of the tallest waterfalls in the Southern Appalachians. The Pigeon Creek Trail to the falls begins at the Mingo Falls Campground. To find the campground, travel south on US 441 from the Oconaluftee Visitor Center and take the second left onto Big Cove Road. In 5 miles turn right and drive in to the campground. A short yet moderate hike leads to the waterfall.

10 Pearson's Falls

2748 Pearson Falls Road, Saluda, NC 28773; 828-749-3031
pearsonsfalls.org

It's a short (0.25-mile) moderate hike to a beautiful payoff: a 90-foot waterfall. The area is well cared for by its owner, the Tryon Garden Club, and covers 275 acres. Closed January, Thanksgiving, and December 25. Admission charged.

Looking Glass Falls is one of 250 waterfalls in Transylvania County, Land of the Waterfalls.

White Bengal tigers, such as this one at Tiger World, are a genetic variation of orange Bengal tigers.

FROM THE BLACK BEARS high atop Grandfather Mountain to the sea turtles that lay their eggs on the North Carolina coast, the state has a rich abundance of wildlife. You might chance upon a bear in the wild in the western part of the state, but there are also many centers, zoos, and rehabilitation facilities where you can get a closer look at various species.

SPEND TIME OUTDOORS:

Wildlife Adventures

Lemurs are native only to Madagascar, but you can see this Coquerel's sifaka at Duke Lemur Center.

1 Aloha Safari Zoo

159 Mini Lane, Cameron, NC 28326; 919-770-7109
alohasafarizoo.org

This 60-plus-acre zoo opened in 2010 as a sanctuary for unwanted, mistreated, and injured animals. Owner Lee Crutchfield built the place himself and cares for a wide variety of species. More than 400 animals—including African crested porcupine, black spider monkey, arctic wolf, dromedary camel, Japanese macaque, kunekune pig, Bengal tiger, red kangaroo, Russian grizzly bear, zebra, and many others—live at this zoo. A safari tour allows you to see and feed the larger animals. Open March–October, Tuesday–Sunday; November–February, Saturday and Sunday only. Admission charged.

2 Carolina Raptor Center

6000 Sample Road, Huntersville, NC 28078; 704-875-6521
carolinaraptorcenter.org

This center began in 1975 when a broad-winged hawk was brought to Dr. Richard Brown, a University of North Carolina at Charlotte ornithologist. Dr. Brown and student Deb Sue Griffin officially founded the Carolina Raptor Center in 1981, and it moved to the Latta Nature Preserve in 1984. Today, it's home to about 100 permanent resident birds, including eagles, hawks, owls, corvids, vultures, and falcons. The Raptor Trail is open March–October, daily, and November–February, Wednesday–Sunday; closed January 1, Easter, Thanksgiving, and December 25. Admission charged.

3 Carolina Tiger Rescue

1940 Hanks Chapel Road, Pittsboro, NC 27312; 919-542-4684
carolinatigerrescue.org

Ten species of animals—including cheetahs, bobcats, lions, tigers, and kinkajous—currently live at Carolina Tiger Rescue. Many of the animals have been rescued from desperate situations and now are cared for within large, natural habitat enclosures. Private tours, twilight tours, tiger tales tours, and special experiences are available. Public tours are offered year-round Friday–Sunday and run an hour and a half. Admission charged.

4 Corolla Wild Horse Tours

1210 Ocean Trail, Corolla, NC 27927; 252-207-0511
seecorollawildhorses.com

The Corolla Wild Horses have a long history at the Outer Banks—they've been roaming the shores since the 1500s when the first Europeans arrived. As the Corolla area developed during the 1980s and 1990s, the numbers of horses declined, but they have risen again after being moved north to Carova Beach. Tours last 2 hours and take guests out in open-air safari-style trucks to places where they can get a glimpse of the horses. Closed Sunday, some Saturdays, and December–February. Admission charged.

5 Deer Park Petting Zoo at Tweetsie Railroad

300 Tweetsie Railroad Lane, Blowing Rock, NC 28605; 800-526-5740
tweetsie.com/explore-the-park/deer-park

More than 90 animals make their home here, including African pygmy goats, European fallow deer, Nubian goats, emus, llamas, burros, miniature horses, micro-mini donkeys, Olde English (Babydoll) Southdown sheep, and yellow-bellied and red-eared slider turtles. Ride the chairlift to the top of Tweetsie Railroad park to access the animal area. A bus also shuttles visitors to the park. Closed January–March; hours vary seasonally, so check the website or call before you go. Admission charged.

6 Duke Lemur Center

3705 Erwin Road, Durham, NC 27705; 919-401-7240
lemur.duke.edu

This center houses 17 species of prosimian primates, including 15 species of lemurs and two species of loris. Reservations are required to visit the lemurs, which are the most endangered group of mammals in the world. There are four options for tours: Lemurs Live (public), Lemurs Live (private), Little Lemurs (children ages 3–8), and Enrichment. Tours are not offered on Tuesdays. Visitors do not have any physical contact with the animals due to safety measures. Closed January 1, Thanksgiving, December 24–25, and occasionally for staff enrichment and private tours. Admission charged.

7 Grandfather Mountain

2050 Blowing Rock Hwy., Linville, NC 28646; 800-468-7325
grandfather.com

The animals here live in large environmental habitats. There are seven habitats in all, featuring such animals as black bears, cougars, bald eagles, elk, and river otters. Special encounters each day provide a chance to see the animals up close. In June each year, there's an

animal birthday party with special events, games, and contests. Closed Thanksgiving, December 25, and during inclement weather. Admission charged.

8 Magic Wings Butterfly House

433 W. Murray Ave., Durham, NC 27704; 919-220-5429
lifeandscience.org/magic-wings

Located in the Museum of Life + Science, the Magic Wings Butterfly House holds daily butterfly releases. This year-round immersive experience gives visitors the chance to witness hundreds of tropical butterflies in a rainforest environment. Magic Wings also includes Bayer Insectarium, which features exotic insects and invertebrates from around the world. Closed Monday from Labor Day to Memorial Day. Admission charged.

9 North Carolina Aquarium at Fort Fisher

900 Loggerhead Road, Kure Beach, NC 28449; 910-772-0500
ncaquariums.com/fort-fisher

Animal encounters allow chances to see the animals up close and ask questions of the staff. Additional tours provide the opportunity to go beyond the normal experience: Behind the Scenes Tour (age 8 and older, 1.5 hours), Extended Behind the Scenes (age 8 and older, 2 hours), Fins and Family Tour (fun learning for families with children ages 3–7, 30 minutes), and Surf Fishing Workshop (age 10 and older, 3 hours). Closed Thanksgiving and December 25. Admission charged.

10 North Carolina Aquarium at Pine Knoll

1 Roosevelt Blvd., Pine Knoll Shores, NC 28512; 252-247-4003
ncaquariums.com/pine-knoll-shores

A key habitat here is The Living Shipwreck, the largest man-made ocean habitat in North Carolina (306,000 gallons). It has a replica of the *U-352* German submarine that the U.S. Coast Guard sunk off the coast of North Carolina in 1942. Animals found here include sandbar sharks, sand tiger sharks, nurse sharks, Atlantic spadefish, and other species. Closed Thanksgiving and December 25. Admission charged.

11 North Carolina Zoo

4401 Zoo Parkway, Asheboro, NC 27205; 800-488-0444
nczoo.org

The North Carolina Zoo has the distinction of being the world's largest natural habitat zoo. This allows its 1,800 resident animals plenty of room to roam and live. A sampling of the animals found here includes Asian fairy bluebirds, grizzly bears, Southern white rhinos, horned puffins, Thomson's gazelles, and red wolves. Closed Thanksgiving and December 25. Admission charged.

12 Sylvan Heights Bird Park

500 Sylvan Heights Park Way, Scotland Neck, NC 27874; 252-826-3186
shwpark.com

First opened in 2006, this 18-acre zoo now contains more than 2,000 waterfowl, flamingos, parrots, toucans, and other birds from around the world. Closed Monday, Thanksgiving, and December 25. Admission charged.

13 Team ECCO Aquarium & Shark Lab

511 N. Main St., Hendersonville, NC 28792; 828-692-8386
teamecco.org

You don't have to go to the coast to learn about sea life. Team ECCO Aquarium & Shark Lab is the first inland aquarium in North Carolina. Owner Brenda B. J. Ramer was teaching school when she realized many of her students couldn't comprehend blue water. "I decided to do more than give them a book and a DVD." She opened a small classroom in 2009 and then expanded to a much larger location in downtown Hendersonville. The facility raises baby sharks for research. They celebrated a miracle birth when a female bamboo shark pup was hatched from a parthenogenesis egg (that's an egg that developed an embryo without fertilization). Closed Sunday–Tuesday. Admission charged.

14 Tiger World

4400 Cook Road, Rockwell, NC 28138; 704-279-6363
tigerworld.us

Tiger World hosts a wide mix of species, including some endangered animals and two species that are extinct from the wild: Barbary lion and Syrian brown bear. It has animals from Africa, Asia, Australia, North America, and South America. Visitors will be able to see them running, eating, sleeping, and having encounters with their handlers. Closed Wednesday, Thanksgiving, and December 25. Admission charged.

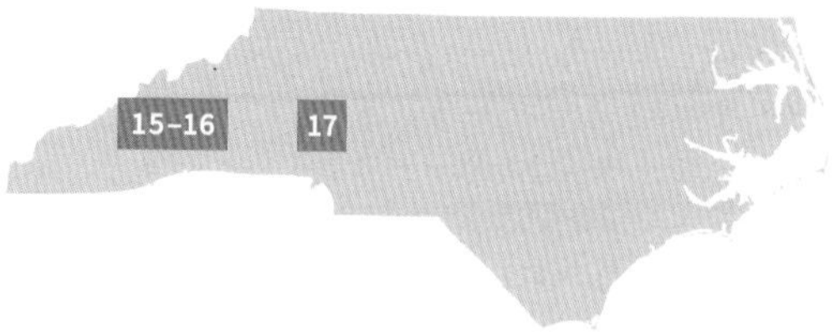

15 Urban Bears

facebook.com/urbanbearstudy

Don't be surprised if you plan a day trip to Asheville and wind up having a real-life bear encounter. Bears have been a fairly constant sight, even in populated areas of Asheville, for some time now. Researchers have been putting GPS collars on some of the bears to track their activity and movements. Check the BearWise website for advice on what to do if you find yourself near a bear: bearwise.org /bear-safety-tips.

16 WNC Nature Center

75 Gashes Creek Road, Asheville, NC 28805; 828-259-8080
wildwnc.org

The newest residents here are a pair of red pandas. They arrived in late 2018 as part of the new Prehistoric Appalachia project. A fun way to connect with the animals here is to adopt one of them. That doesn't mean they go home with you—it simply means you have a new wildlife friend and your support goes toward habitat improvement. Other animals found here include bears, cougars, bobcats, gray wolves, goats, sheep, owls, hawks, otters, raccoons, snakes, and more. Closed January 1, Thanksgiving, and December 24–25. Admission charged.

17 Zootastic Park

385 Ostwalt Amity Road, Troutman, NC 28115; 704-245-6446
zootasticpark.com

This private zoo houses a wide variety of animals—everything from kangaroos to primates to tigers. Take advantage of the unique options for hands-on encounters with the animals (for an additional fee). Open daily. Admission charged.

Black bears are a common sight in Asheville, even in urban areas.

Climb 200 steps to reach the top of Bodie Island Light Station, built in 1872.

BELIEVE IT OR NOT, North Carolina's beaches aren't just found on the coast—the mountains also feature a couple: Lake Lure Beach and Lake Powhatan Beach. Of course, those two are lakefront beaches. To find the traditional beaches, head east to the coastline and/or visit the Outer Banks.

SPEND TIME OUTDOORS:
Beaches & Lighthouses

Beaches

Atlantic Beach
atlanticbeach-nc.com; 252-726-2121

Bald Head Island
villagebhi.org; 910-457-9700

Brunswick Islands
ncbrunswick.com; 910-755-5517

Carolina Beach
carolinabeach.org; 910-458-2999

Currituck Beach
visitcurrituck.com; 252-435-2947

Emerald Isle
crystalcoastnc.org/region/emerald-isle; 252-393-2008

Holden Beach
ncbrunswick.com/islands/holden-beach; 910-755-5517

Kure Beach
townofkurebeach.org; 910-458-8216

Lake Lure
lakeluretours.com; 828-625-1373

Lake Powhatan
pisgahhospitalitypartners.com/lake-powhatan; 877-444-6777

Oak Island
ncbrunswick.com/islands/oak-island; 910-755-5517

Ocracoke Island
visitocracokenc.com; 252-928-6711

Beaches *(continued)*

Outer Banks
outerbanks.org; 877-629-4386

Topsail Beach
topsailbeach.org; 910-328-5841

Wrightsville Beach
wilmingtonandbeaches.com/wrightsville-beach; 877-406-2356

Beaches & Lighthouses

Lighthouses

Bodie Island Light Station
8210 Bodie Island Lighthouse Road, Nags Head, NC 27959; 252-473-2111
nps.gov/caha/planyourvisit/bils.htm

Cape Hatteras Lighthouse
46379 Lighthouse Road, Buxton, NC 27920; 252-473-2111
nps.gov/caha/planyourvisit/chls.htm

Currituck Beach Light Station
1101 Corolla Village Road, Corolla, NC 27927; 252-453-4939
currituckbeachlight.com

Frying Pan Tower
32.5 miles southeast of Bald Head Island in the Atlantic Ocean (GPS: N33° 29.000' W77° 35.000'); 704-907-0399; fptower.com

Oak Island Lighthouse
1100 Caswell Beach Road, Caswell Beach, NC 28465; oakislandlighthouse.org

Ocracoke Lighthouse
Lighthouse Road, Ocracoke, NC 27960; 252-473-2111
nps.gov/caha/planyourvisit/ols.htm

Old Baldy Lighthouse
Bald Head Island, accessibly only by boat (address for ferry: 1301 Ferry Road, Southport, NC 28461); 910-457-7481; oldbaldy.org

Roanoke Marshes Lighthouse
104 Fernando St., Manteo, NC 27954
outerbanks.com/roanoke-marshes-lighthouse.html; 252-475-1750

Roanoke River Lighthouse, Edenton
Edenton, NC 27932 (GPS: N36° 03.349' W76° 36.587'); 252-482-7800
edentonlighthouse.org

Roanoke River Lighthouse, Plymouth
215 W. Water St., Plymouth, NC 27962; 252-217-2204
roanokeriverlighthouse.com

Fish from the pier or simply take in the vistas at Wrightsville Beach.

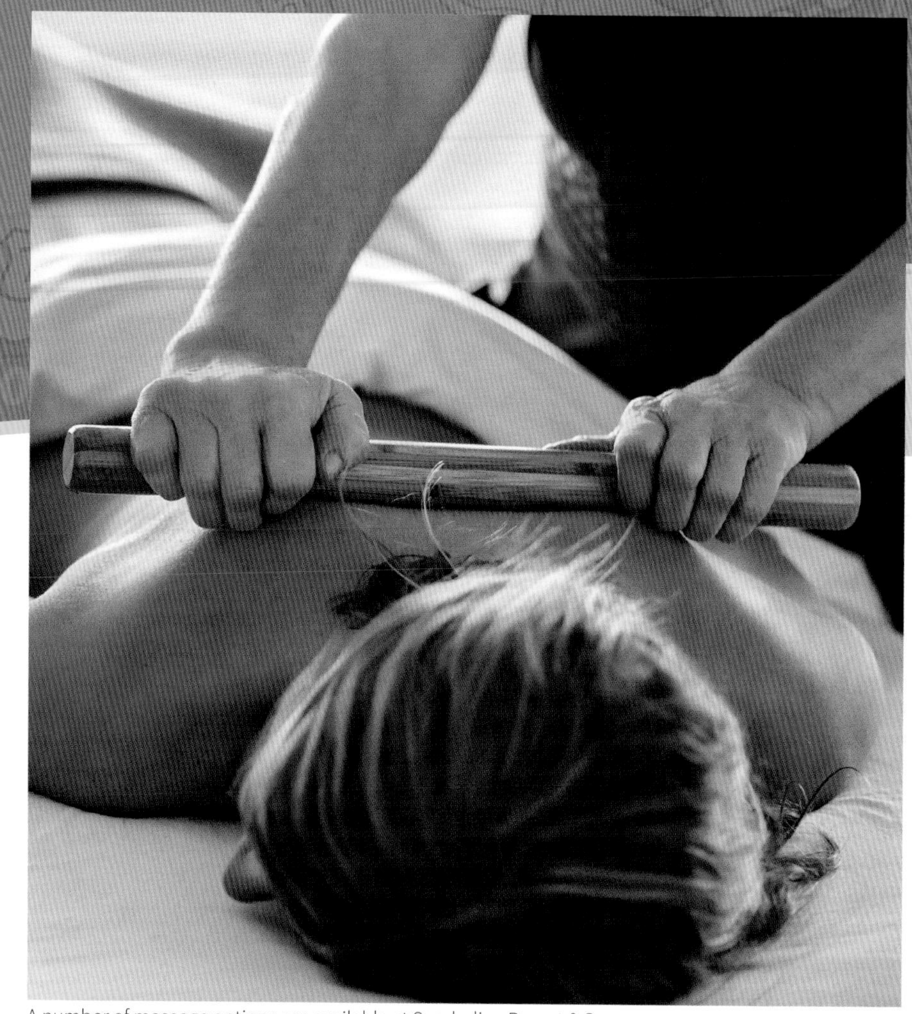

A number of massage options are available at Sanderling Resort & Spa.
(courtesy of Sanderling Resort & Spa)

WHEN WAS THE LAST TIME you carved out a day trip focused simply on self care? While North Carolina offers a myriad of chances to be active and on the go, there are also opportunities to unwind, relax, and take time to engage in treatments that will help you feel your best.

OTHER DAY TRIPS:

Spas & Wellness Retreats

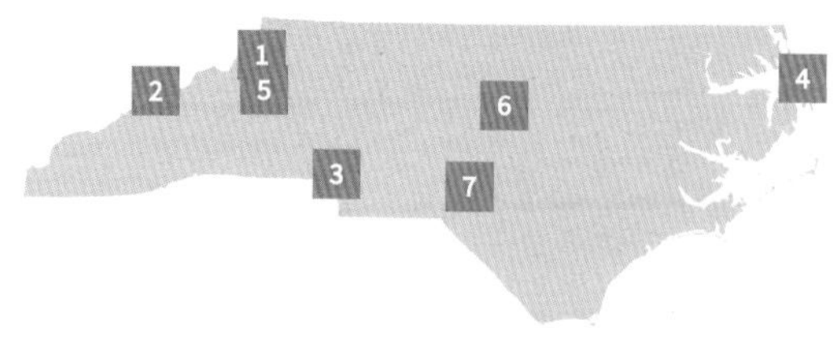

1 The Art of Living Retreat Center Shankara Ayurveda Spa

639 Whispering Hills Road, Boone, NC 28607; 828-264-8382
artoflivingretreatcenter.org/spa

As its name indicates, the Shankara Ayurveda Spa at the Art of Living Retreat Center features Ayurvedic treatments. If you're feeling frazzled from a busy life, check out Shirodhara: Relaxation Therapy, where a therapist pours a continuous stream of warm oil on your forehead. Other treatments include help with settling the nervous system and nasal therapy. If you have time for more than a day trip, check out the variety of getaways, including Weekends of Creativity, where you can take pottery classes, as well as engage in progressive meditation and yoga.

2 Hot Springs Resort and Spa

315 Bridge St., Hot Springs, NC 28743; 828-622-7676
nchotsprings.com/spa-services

I highly recommend this experience, which is a personal favorite. Soak in a hot tub filled with naturally warm mineral water beside the banks of the French Broad River and Spring Creek. The water is between 100°F and 104°F. It's an ultra-relaxing way to spend an hour. Then, if you want additional pampering, sign up for a therapeutic massage.

3 The Ritz-Carlton Spa, Charlotte

201 E. Trade St., Charlotte, NC 28202; 704-547-2244
ritzcarlton.com/en/hotels/charlotte/spa

This upscale day spa offers five treatment rooms, women's and men's lounges, a fitness center, a pool, a hot tub, a nail salon, and a pink Himalayan salt room. Check out the Honey and Chocolate Detox Ritual or the Ultimate Chocolate and Honey Pedicure. The spa is open to people age 18 and older; the salon is open to all ages.

4 Sanderling Resort & Spa

1461 Duck Road, Duck, NC 27949; 855-412-7866
sanderling-resort.com/spa.php

Signature Treatments here create a special connection with the environment as therapists incorporate ingredients from the Outer Banks. One example is the Sea Creations Facial with a serum applied with a tiger conch shell. Choose among a full menu of relaxing massages, facials, body care, and more.

5 The Spa at Chetola Resort

185 Chetola Lake Dr., Blowing Rock, NC 28605; 828-295-5531
chetola.com/spa

Opened in 2009, this spa is comprised of five treatment rooms; a relaxation room; a nail treatment area; and the Swan Bar, which is stocked with complimentary teas, coffees, and homemade granola. A special Spa Daycation package is offered November–April, Sunday–Thursday. Spa packages are available with or without overnight accommodations. The spa is open to children ages 12–18 with a signed waiver and parent attendance, and children ages 8–11 have access to salon services with a signed waiver and parental attendance.

6 The Spa at Fearrington

2000 Fearrington Village Center, Pittsboro, NC 27312; 919-545-5723
fearrington.com/spa

If you have the time and money, carve out half a day to enjoy The Ultimate Experience. It includes a 30-minute salt scrub, a 60-minute Swedish massage, a 60-minute facial, a manicure, and a pedicure. Other packages, including a couple's massage, and à la carte treatments are available. Take time to explore the Fearrington Gardens—open daily.

7 The Spa at Pinehurst

80 Carolina Vista, Pinehurst, NC 28374; 855-235-8507
pinehurst.com/spa

Cryotherapy is among the menu options here. This treatment cools the skin's exterior layer with subzero air, stimulating the body and causing the release of those feel-good endorphins. Other services include massages, nail care, facials, and specialty services like the contouring seaweed body wrap. Pinehurst has a rich golfing history and has hosted the U.S. Open three times.

8 The Spa at the Inn at Biltmore Estate

1 Lodge St., Asheville, NC 28803; 828-225-6772
biltmore.com/stay/inn/spa

The Signature Estate Experience lasts 2 hours and includes a full body exfoliation, a warm body wrap with heated stones, an aromatherapy scalp treatment, and a massage. Various massage, beauty, and skin care packages and individual services are provided. Spa services are offered to overnight guests and Biltmore annual pass holders.

9 The Spa at the Omni Grove Park Inn

290 Macon Ave., Asheville, NC 28804; 800-438-5800
omnihotels.com/hotels/asheville-grove-park/spa

The incredible 43,000-square-foot facility provides the ultimate in relaxation. Along with a wide variety of spa services, take time to enjoy the mineral pools with piped-in underwater music and nearby waterfall pools. Soak in the beauty of Asheville at the outdoor hot tub and fireplace. Day passes are open to overnight resort guests only, age 18 and older.

10 Westglow Resort & Spa

224 Westglow Cir., Blowing Rock, NC 28605; 828-295-4463
westglowresortandspa.com/spa

Check out the day spa packages that allow you to customize your experience with a variety of wellness, body, face, salon, or fitness options. The price includes access to all the spa resort facilities—an indoor swimming pool, a hot tub, a sauna, a steam room, a weight room, a cardiovascular center, a relaxation lounge, and a tennis court. Guided hikes are available, and the poolside café serves a gourmet lunch.

At the Ritz-Carlton, Charlotte, take a dip in the spa's pool in the Aqua Lounge. (courtesy of the Ritz-Carlton, Charlotte)

Search for interesting finds at an antiques mall.
(photographed by Marla Milling)

IF YOU LONG FOR A PIECE OF THE PAST, North Carolina offers an abundance of antiques stores that sell a wide variety of vintage items—everything from Pyrex bowls to metal toys and more. The thrill of the hunt is part of the fun. My motto: "I don't know what I'm looking for until I find it." Chart out a course by reviewing the member listings on northcarolinaantiquetrail.com. I've picked out a few favorites to get you started.

OTHER DAY TRIPS: Antiques & Junk

Antiques Stores

Antique Market of Shelby
323 E. Marion St., Shelby, NC 28150; 980-404-1117; antiquemarketofshelby.com

Antique Tobacco Barn
75 Swannanoa River Road, Asheville, NC 28805; 828-252-7291; atbarn.com

Balsam Antique Mall
10 Balsam Ridge Road, Waynesville, NC 28786; 828-452-7070; balsamantiquemall.com

Franklin's Antique Mall
215 E. Front St., New Bern, NC 28560; 252-631-5210; franklinsantiquemall.com

Front Porch Antique Market
8807 NC 105 S, Boone, NC 28607; 828-963-7450; frontporchantiquemarket.com

Granddaddy's Antique Mall
2316 Maple Ave., Burlington, NC 27215; 336-570-1997; granddaddys.com

Michael Moore Antiques
539 Castle St., Wilmington, NC 28401; 910-763-0300; michaelmooreantiquesnc.com

The Old Mill Antiques
204 E. Main St., Glen Alpine, NC 28628; 828-584-4550; theoldmillantiquesnc.com

Village Green Antiques Mall
424 N. Main St., Hendersonville, NC 28792; 828-692-9057; villagegreenantiquemall.com

Flea Markets

Brightleaf Flea Market
2320 S. Brightleaf Blvd., Smithfield, NC 27577; 919-934-4111; brightleaffleamarket.com

Farmers Market Flea Market
366 Livestock Market Road, Lexington, NC 27295; 336-479-0334
farmersmarket-fleamarketnc.com

Flea Markets *(continued)*

Jamestown Flea Market

709 Jamestown Road, Morganton, NC 28655; 828-584-4038
jamestownfleamarket.net

Raleigh Flea Market

1025 Blue Ridge Road, Raleigh, NC 27607; 919-899-FLEA (3532)
raleighfleamarket.net

Smiley's Flea Market

5360 Hendersonville Road, Fletcher, NC 28732; 828-684-3532
smileysfleamarkets.com/north-carolina

Uncle Bill's Flea Market

5427 US 74 W, Whittier, NC 28789; 828-586-9613
unclebillsfleamarket.com

Webb Road Flea Market

905 Webb Road, Salisbury, NC 28146; 704-857-6660
webbroadmarket.com

Thrift Shops

Bargain Box—The Junior League of Greensboro

1410 Mill St., Greensboro, NC 27408; 336-273-6349
bargainboxofgreensboro.org

Class and Trash

906 S. Croatan Hwy, Kill Devil Hills, NC 27948; 252-715-4412
classandtrash.com

The Coalition Resale Shops

1117 W. Pennsylvania Ave., Southern Pines, NC 28387; 910-693-1600
sandhillscoalition.org/resale-shops-donation-center/the-shops

Four Seasons Hospice Home Store

215 N. Main St., Hendersonville, NC 28792; 828-696-0625
fourseasonscfl.org/how-you-can-help/hospice-home-store

Habitat for Humanity ReStores

Various locations across North Carolina
habitat.org/restores

HANDmeUPs Thrift Store

8320 Litchford Road, #102, Raleigh, NC 27615; 919-876-5750
handmeupsthrift.org

Second Chances Thrift Shop

49 Glendale Ave., Asheville, NC 28803; 828-505-2017
bwar.org/second-chances

Winston-Salem Rescue Mission Thrift Store

704 Oak St. NW, Winston-Salem, NC 27101; 336-723-1848
wsrescue.org/thrift-store

INDEX

D

E

F

G

M

N

S

T

U

Check out this great title from
Menasha Ridge Press!

North Carolina Adventure Weekends

Jessie Johnson and Matt Schneider
ISBN: 978-1-63404-092-1
$16.95, 1st Edition

5.5 x 8.5, paperback
216 pages, full color
maps and photos

Each chapter in this full-color guide highlights a focused geographic area and includes detailed directions, so readers can spend more time playing and less time driving from place to place. Adventurers will also learn where to stock up on supplies, what to do on a rainy day, and where to go to rehash the weekend's adventures over a meal and a beer.

Inside you'll find trip descriptions to the 12 best destinations for weekend adventures rated for difficulty. You'll also find lodging options, restaurants, breweries, coffee shops, and ideal outings for individuals, couples, families, and groups.